Sing a Song for Sixpence

SING A SONG for SIXPENCE

THE ENGLISH PICTURE-BOOK TRADITION AND RANDOLPH CALDECOTT

BRIAN ALDERSON

Cambridge University Press
in association with the British Library

Catalogue of an exhibition held at the British Library
October 1986–January 1987.

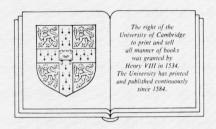

The right of the
University of Cambridge
to print and sell
all manner of books
was granted by
Henry VIII in 1534.
The University has printed
and published continuously
since 1584.

Published by the Press Syndicate of the University
of Cambridge.
The Pitt Building, Trumpington Street, Cambridge
CB2 1RP
32 East 57th Street, New York, NY 10022, USA
10 Stamford Road, Oakleigh, Melbourne 3166,
Australia

© Cambridge University Press and the British
Library Board, 1986

First published 1986

Produced by
The British Library
Great Russell Street
London WC1B 3DG

Editor: David Way
Designer: Roger Davies

British Library Cataloguing in Publication Data
Alderson, Brian
    Sing a song for sixpence : the English picture
    book tradition and Randolph Caldecott
    1. Picture-books for children—
    Bibliography—Catalogs
    I. Title   II. British Library
    011′.625054   Z1037
    ISBN 0–521–33179–X
    ISBN 0–521–33760–7 Pbk

Library of Congress Cataloging in Publication Data
Alderson, Brian.
    Sing a song for sixpence.
    "Catalogue of an exhibiton held at the British
Library, October 1986–January 1987"—t.p. verso.
    I. Illustrated books, Children's—England—
Exhibitions. 2. Picture-books for children—
England—Exhibitions.   3. Caldecott, Randolph,
1846–1886—Exhibitions.   4. Illustration of
books—England—Exhibitions. 5. Bibliographical
exhibitions—England—London. 6. Children's
literature, English—Bibliography—Exhibitions.
I. British Library.   II. Title.
Z1037.A39   1986
[PN1009.A1]   011′.62   86.14788
ISBN 0–521–33179–X hard covers
ISBN 0–521–33760–7 paperback

Typeset by August Filmsetting, Haydock, St. Helens
Printed in Great Britain by Ebenezer Baylis & Son Ltd
The Trinity Press, Worcester and London

Contents page illustration: from Thomas
Rowlandson's *Characteristic Sketches of the
Lower Orders* (London, 1819).
BL, C.55 cc–1(2).

For Chris

Half-title illustration

*Catalogue of a Loan Collection of the Works of
Randolph Caldecott at the Brasenose Club, with a
memoir by George Evans*
Manchester, John Heywood, 1888. Picture size
5 × 3½ in. Line block of an engraving by Henry
Watkinson, after a photograph

Caldecott's widow writes of this portrait: '...
Besides the one in Mr Blackburn's "Memoir",
which many like, and that in the *Graphic*, there
is one other, of which I am sending you a
copy. It is the one I think the best, but some
people do not like it because the expression is
too grave, they consider, and he looks ill. It is,
however, exactly like my husband'.

BL. 7858 bb 48 p.[26]

Cover and title-page illustrations from Randolph
Caldecott's *Sing a song for sixpence* (Routledge,
[1878]).

Contents

Randolph Caldecott, 'artist and illustrator', died in St Augustine, Florida, on the night of 12 February 1886. Never very strong in health, he was wintering in the Southern United States when an unusually cold spell struck Florida and he succumbed to heart-failure after a wretched illness. He was thirty-nine years old.

Despite the constant uncertainty of his health, Caldecott lived this short life with an enviable zest and good humour. He was born at Chester on 22 March 1846, the son of a hatter (though a gloss of respectability has been put on this, and 'accountant' is sometimes said). He seems to have spent a fairly idyllic boyhood in comfortable circumstances, and even when he entered the rather cramping trade of banking—first at Whitchurch, then in Manchester—his cheerful spirits flourished. He had an invigorating circle of friends who (along with everyone else) encouraged his natural talents as an artist, and when he gave up clerking and moved to London in order to make a living by his art he endured the heavy working schedule that that entailed with a typical buoyancy:

I have just got into a new workshop next door at the back, and there I light my stove and carry on my business. Do you want a signboard? or an equestrian statue? or an elegant wallpaper? Anything in that line I shall be happy to attend to, and hope that by a steady &c. &c, to merit a continuance of that &c, &c, which the nobility, clergy, &c, &c, have for so many &c so liberally &c, &c.   (*Letter to William Etches, 1 January 1874.*)

Caldecott's relish for comedy and for the traditions of English rural life is the quality most evident in the book-illustrations that brought him fame when he was thirty: a set of one hundred and twenty drawings engraved on wood by the veteran engraver James Cooper, for an edition of Washington Irving's *Old Christmas* (Macmillan, 1876). By this time he had already had many cartoons and drawings published in the illustrated papers of the day, *Punch* included, but from 1876 to his early death his work was much in demand from all quarters.

We can see from his published correspondence and from what remains of his preparatory sketches and his proof-corrected drawings that he was both a severe self-critic and a shrewd manager of his own business affairs. (That training in the bank was not in vain.)

Among the large output of drawings, paintings, decorative-work and book-illustrations that he completed, it is now the 'Caldecott Toy Books' that are paramount. He negotiated a scheme for these with the famous colour-

Charles H. Bennett (ed.)
The Old Nurse's Book of Rhymes, Jingles and Ditties, edited and illustrated by Charles H. Bennett. With ninety engravings.
London, Griffith and Farran, 1858. Hand-coloured wood engraving. Frontispiece.
BL. 12807, f.70.

printer Edmund Evans about 1877, when Evans was also sponsoring the early published work of Kate Greenaway. This scheme led to, or was supported by, a set of water-colour drawings for the first two suggested books: *The House that Jack Built* and *The Diverting History of John Gilpin*. Edmund Evans, who was well able to tell a hawk from a hand-saw, accepted the idea and in the autumn of 1878 these two picture books were published by George Routledge and Sons in an edition of some 10,000 copies each,

Their success was immediate. Reviewers were enthusiastic: '*the* book for children', said *Punch* on December 14, 1878; 'the very essence of all illustration for children's books', said *The Times* on Christmas Eve, and echoed to the praise of W.E. Henley in the *Academy* of November 16, who remarked that 'Mr Caldecott is of the rare artists who never waste a stroke, who give you in a dozen scratches the effect that some men fail to produce by an elaborate system of composition and design.'

Caldecott reported from Cannes on December 13 that he was being asked by fellow guests in his hotel if he were related to 'the gifted artist'. He added that 30,000 copies of each book were delivered up to Christmas and (optimistically) that another 20,000 were expected to sell soon after.

From this time up to his death Caldecott produced two Toy Books a year and this small collection of sixteen books represents both a culmination in the Victorian craft of picture-book making and a model for the blending of words and pictures in books for young children. The praise of contemporary lay-critics was echoed by Caldecott's fellow-professionals (not always a natural reaction among artistic brethren) and more recent practitioners of the art of the picture book, from Beatrix Potter and Leslie Brooke to Edward Ardizzone, have acknowledged his pre-eminence. In the United States the major annual award for picture books is named after him—the American Library Association Caldecott Medal; his three jovial huntsmen were in 1924 neatly adopted as an emblem for the leading review journal of children's books, the *Horn Book Magazine*; and there has been no better assessment of the qualities of his books than that given in a series of critical parerga by the American illustrator Maurice Sendak, quotations from which turn up with monotonous regularity in the following pages.

This book has been prepared on the occasion of an exhibition at the British Library prompted in the first place by a wish to commemorate the centenary of the death of this beneficent artist. The aim however is not to present a full coverage of his achievement (for this was admirably carried out in the fine Caldecott Exhibition mounted at Manchester City Art Gallery in 1977–78). Instead an opportunity has been taken to try to place his work within the tradition of narrative illustration and to show how he figures as *primus inter pares* in an essentially English style in the creation of children's picture books. Chauvinistically or not, one can argue that this 'English' style is a touchstone for the judging of all picture-book art, embodying as it does a flexible and richly responsive interplay between text and illustration with an emphasis throughout on the quality of line rather than on less essential features of *chiaroscouro* and colouring. Both book and exhibition are not so much chronological descriptions as ruminations on one of our happiest and most fruitful contributions to a small but significant art form.

Washington Irving
Old Christmas ... illustrated by R. Caldecott.
London, Macmillan & Co., 1876. Picture size
5¼ × 2 in. Wood engraving by J.D. Cooper after a
drawing by R.C.
BL. 12703 bbb 2 p.154

Maurice Sendak [and Randolph Caldecott]
Cover illustration for the *Horn Book Magazine*
Vol 61, no. 6.

(Boston, November, 1985). Picture size 5¼ × 6 in.
Photo-litho reproduction of a water-colour drawing.

The centre-piece for this composite set of
visual quotations is Sendak's copy of a
drawing which Caldecott made while working
with Henry Blackburn on the book *Breton Folk*
(London, 1880). It was called, appropriately
enough, 'Sketching under difficulties'.

Reproduced by permission of *Horn Book Magazine*.

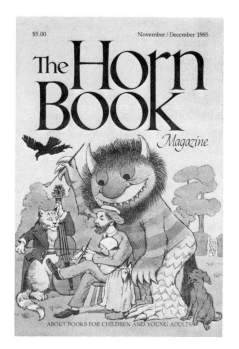

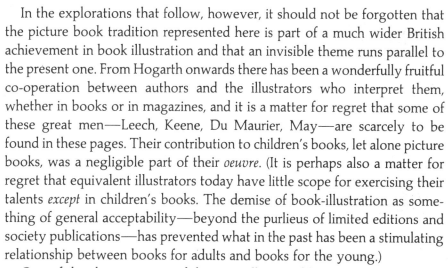

Caldecott Medal
Obverse of the Caldecott Medal, awarded
annually for the most distinguished picture
book published in the United States during the
previous year. The design is by René Paul
Chambellan using a motif from Caldecott's
John Gilpin.

Reproduced with permission of the American
Library Association.

In the explorations that follow, however, it should not be forgotten that
the picture book tradition represented here is part of a much wider British
achievement in book illustration and that an invisible theme runs parallel to
the present one. From Hogarth onwards there has been a wonderfully fruitful
co-operation between authors and the illustrators who interpret them,
whether in books or in magazines, and it is a matter for regret that some of
these great men—Leech, Keene, Du Maurier, May—are scarcely to be
found in these pages. Their contribution to children's books, let alone picture
books, was a negligible part of their *oeuvre*. (It is perhaps also a matter for
regret that equivalent illustrators today have little scope for exercising their
talents *except* in children's books. The demise of book-illustration as something of general acceptability—beyond the purlieus of limited editions and
society publications—has prevented what in the past has been a stimulating
relationship between books for adults and books for the young.)

One of the characteristics of the great illustrated books is, of course, the
working together of text and image *seriatim*, and this makes for difficulties in
discussing them either as examples in a book or as items in an exhibition. To
judge them fully it is necessary to read them from end to end and to observe
how words and pictures run together throughout. Such an indulgence is not
possible with many of the rare and often fragile works described here (some
of which are themselves in rather sad condition through much use by readers
over several generations) but an effort has been made to select page-
openings that will fairly represent the style of a particular book and may at
the same time allow for useful comparisons with similar subjects. It should
also be pointed out, first, that in some instances a page-opening has been
chosen for reproduction in this book that is different from the one on exhibition; and, second, that some of the books illustrated are ones for which no
place could be found in the exhibition.

Even so, it must be recognised that what is set out here is only a tiny fragment of a multi-faceted subject. A dozen books could often have been chosen instead of one to demonstrate or refine a point—especially where the prolific output of the present day is concerned. But the form of this essay and the examples assembled within it are chiefly there to define and celebrate a tradition. It is my hope that we shall continue to recognise the vitality of that tradition—and thereby to honour the central place within it of Randolph Caldecott.

Brian Alderson
Westwood, Los Angeles
March 1986

Photograph of a rubbing of Caldecott's gravestone in the cemetery at St. Augustine, Florida. (Reproduced from a rubbing in the De Grammond Collection at the University of Southern Mississippi.) Alongside at left is placed a picture of another Caldecott family gravestone, cheerfully portrayed by the artist himself in *The Fox Jumps over the Parson's Gate* (London, George Routledge & Sons, n.d.).

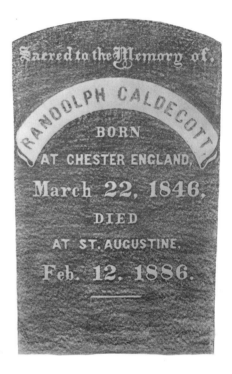

A note on illustrations and dating

The illustrations have been chosen in order to clarify or expand upon matters raised in the main text. An attempt has been made to annotate them systematically, most notes consisting of the following elements:

Title: Where illustrations are taken from manuscripts or printed books the title given is that on the title page, or cover where no title-page exists, or in a related colophon.

Date: Publishers of popular and children's books, especially in the nineteenth century, had no consideration for the finicky needs of modern bibliographers, and many of their publications carry no date. When this occurs, conjectural dates have been given in brackets, derived either from the British Library catalogue or from evidence in more recent documentation on the subject.

Size: Most illustrations have had to be reduced in size, and one or two (regrettably) enlarged to meet exigencies of design. The page-size of the original, or, in some cases, of the art-work only, has been given in inches. This civilised, traditional form of measurement has been adopted because it was the one in use when most of the material shown here was being manufactured.

Reproductive methods: Part of the intention of this book is to emphasize a relationship between an illustrator's original work and the methods available to him for its reproduction. A note has therefore been given of the way in which the printed originals of those items illustrated were reproduced. For a number of works — especially nineteenth-century colour illustrations — this has not been easy, for the printers at that time of busy technological innovation left few accounts of how they achieved their often complex illustrative effects. In these instances the technical descriptions should be taken as tentative.

Annotation: An explanation of the purpose of the illustration has been given unless this is clear from the accompanying main text.

Source: Most examples are from the British Library's collections. Shelf-marks or manuscript references are given for these, and sources for those items brought in from elsewhere.

Names and dates: In order not to interrupt the text with a spatter of bracketted numerals, the dating of artists and their works follows no consistent formula.

Acknowledgements

As the by-line to the Preface may suggest, this book has been compiled under slightly unusual circumstances. Between the initial planning of the exhibition and its setting-up I had to undertake a spell of teaching at the University of California at Los Angeles, which resulted in much of the present work being written some 6,000 miles from home-base.

However, if one cannot write about Caldecott in London then there can be few better alternative places than Southern California. Not only have I benefitted from being able to use the splendid collections at the UCLA Research Library and at the Huntington Library, but I have also been within easy distance of two of the finest Caldecott collections in private hands.

Indeed, the wealth of material that has been placed at my disposal, and the hospitality that I have been shown, have perforce directed my attention to the irony that one may now more fruitfully study the splendours of English children's literature in the United States than in England. It is signally depressing to the Englishman that such great collections as those at UCLA, at the Huntington Library, at the University of Indiana at Bloomington, at the Pierpont Morgan Library and at the New York Public Library (to name but a few), have been filled with treasures which so many of the academic and special libraries in Britain have decided are beneath their dignity,.

In acknowledging the extensive help that I have received in working on both the exhibition and this book I should therefore like first of all to name transatlantic friends: Onva Boshears and Jeannine Laughlin at the University of Southern Mississippi, in whose DeGrummond Collection I was able to give thought to the general plan of the exhibition and where I was attentively helped by the librarian, John Kelly; David Zeidberg, who made me so welcome in the Special Collections division of the UCLA Research Library and who allowed me to take up so much of the time of Jim Davis, for whom no query was too trivial for his eager attention. Also in California I must thank especially Gail and Wally Klemm and Myra Cohn Livingston for letting me roam through their Caldecottiana; Kaye MacDonald and Judith Kantor of the University Elementary School; Robert Wark of the Huntington Library and Art Gallery; Rita Lipkis and Chris Olson of the Beverly Hills Public Library; and Cathy Smoyer, *chauffeuse-extraordinaire*. Only Caldecott himself could do justice to the help I received in the way of tables, typewriters, books and moral support from Pat, Bill and Sue Schaefer, ably assisted by Wootton-Briggs and Fitzbilly.

Like so many other collectors and enthusiasts I have also received abundant advice and help in obscure bibliographical points from Justin Schiller of New York—who has, alas, so recently dispersed his own splendid Charles Bennett collection to which the section in this book owes so much. Equally, Jack and Linda Lapides have added to kindnesses given in Baltimore by giving permission for us to use a photograph of *their* unique copy of *Billy Hog*.

In England my first debt is to Elaine Paintin, the British Library's Exhibitions Officer, who from the first was so enthusiastic about the planning of the exhibition; and within the British Library I have received far more help than I delinquently deserve from Anne De Lara, Alan Sterenberg, and David Way, who together with Rosemary Davidson and John Trevitt of Cambridge University Press, have coped so well with the long-distance composition of this book. I am also grateful for help received from Andrew Prescott and Sally Brown of the Department of Manuscripts, and from Paul Goldman of the British Museum's Department of Prints and Drawings.

Beyond Great Russell Street my thanks must go to Tessa Chester of the Museum of Childhood's Renier Collection for her constant encouragement; to Lionel Lambourne of the Victoria & Albert Museum's Department of Prints and Drawings; and to those good friends whose love for this subject is mirrored in their own collections: Marjorie Moon and Iona Opie.

This publication would probably never have seen the light of day if it had not been for the (fairly) tolerant support of my son John, who held intruders at bay, and my wife Valerie, who typed up an illegible manuscript while suffering from a particularly malevolent Southern Californian virus.

Illustration acknowledgements

Thanks are due to the following for giving their permission to reproduce copyright material:

Arts Council; Ernest Benn, now A & C Black (Publishers) Ltd; The Bodley Head; Jonathan Cape Ltd; William Collins Sons & Co. Ltd; Faber and Faber Ltd; Fiona French; William Heinemann Ltd; Penguin Books Ltd; Laurence Pollinger Ltd; Sotheby Parke Bernet Ltd.

Thanks too to Mrs Pat Garrett of Dewhurst St Mary Infants School, Cheshunt, for making available drawings by her pupils.

1

The urge to illustrate

If nature doesn't like a vacuum then human nature doesn't like blank spaces. Set before it a cave-wall, or a hoarding, or a sheet of blotting-paper, and it will get to work with pigments, or spray-cans, or ball-point pens and the offending blankness will be filled.

There is no categorizing what the individual response to this challenge to self-expression will be. It can range from the spontaneous and verbal ('Ghengis Khan but Immanuel Kant') to the stylised and ritualistic (the paintings of Altamira); from the crudely propagandist ('What we want is Watneys') to the elaborately decorative (oases painted on the sides of houses, in Bethnal Green); but the likelihood is that much of it will involve some kind of pictorial comment on a recognisable subject. It will be the expression in drawn-lines of something that might otherwise be expressed in words. It will be illustration.

Here too, though, the scope for variation is enormous. A child may be given a sheet of paper and told to draw the picture of a well-known nursery-rhyme, and out will come a notable cow jumping over an unmistakeable moon (**1**). Another child will be seized with all-too-comprehensible boredom at the longueurs of Latin grammar and will fall to a private commentary on his mentors (**2**). Later in life the same compulsion to off-the-cuff illustration may extend itself beyond committee-room doodles, which have something of the same despairing levity as the schoolboy's marginalia, to, say, private correspondence or the throwing-off of sketches as casual entertainment (**3**).

Alongside these individual and more or less unpremeditated responses

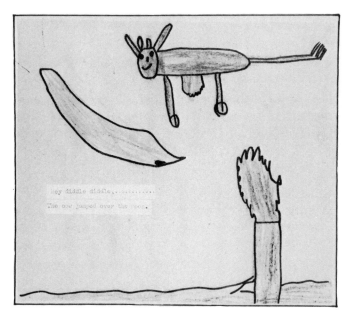

1 Carl Roberts?
The Cow Jumped Over the Moon
$7\frac{1}{2} \times 8\frac{1}{2}$ in. Crayon on paper.

2 William Makepeace Thackeray
Two drawings which he is said to have made in his schoolbooks.
Line block reproduced from G. Everitt's *English Caricaturists* (London, 1885).
BL. 7855, ff.39.

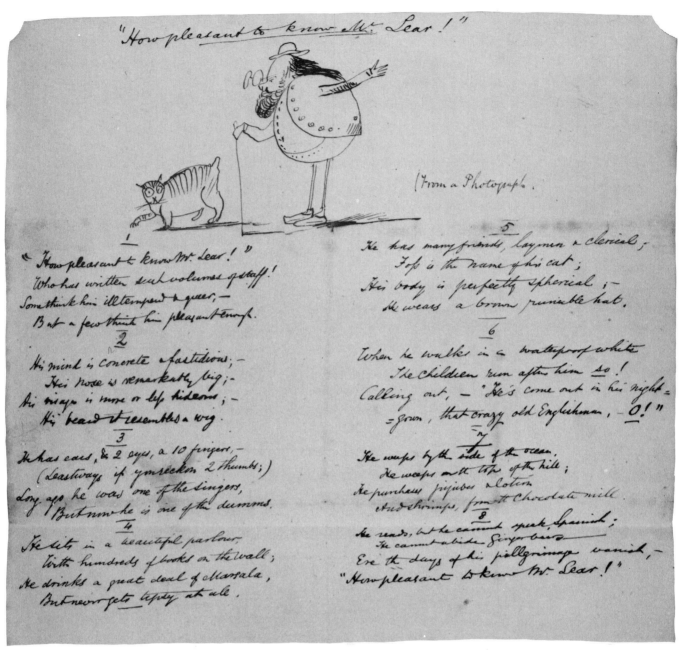

"How pleasant to know Mr. Lear!"

(From a Photograph.)

1
"How pleasant to know Mr. Lear!"
Who has written such volumes of stuff!
Some think him ill-tempered & queer, —
But a few think him pleasant enough.

2
His mind is concrete & fastidious; —
His nose is remarkably big; —
His visage is more or less hideous; —
His beard it resembles a wig.

3
He has ears, & 2 eyes, a 10 fingers, —
(Leastways if you reckon 2 thumbs;)
Long ago he was one of the singers,
But now he is one of the dumms.

4
He sits in a beautiful parlour,
With hundreds of books on the wall;
He drinks a great deal of Marsala,
But never gets tipsy at all.

5
He has many friends, laymen & clerical;
Foss is the name of his cat;
His body is perfectly spherical; —
He wears a brown runcible hat.

6
When he walks in a waterproof white
The children run after him so!
Calling out, — "He's come out in his night-
-gown, that crazy old Englishman, — O!"

7
He weeps by the side of the ocean,
He weeps on the top of the hill;
He purchases pancakes & lotion
And shrimps, from the Chocolate mill.

8
He reads, but he cannot speak Spanish;
He cannot abide ginger-beer:
Ere the days of his pilgrimage vanish, —
"How pleasant to know Mr. Lear!"

however there can also be set the long-standing urge to formalize the relationship between word and picture on a grander scale: preparing sequences of images to accompany a given text with some expectation of a more than private readership. The prevalence of such illustrations throughout history and in many parts of the world is evidence enough of the naturalness of this response,[1] whether it be channeled in a strict tribal tradition or proliferate into some wider movement, producing, say, the splendours and naïvetes of mediaeval book decoration in Western Europe (**4**).

The making of manuscript books, free from the interference of intrusive editors and printers, presents almost ideal conditions for the working out of a closely integrated, but flexible, sequence of narrative events and pictorial interpretations. Evidence survives of such endeavours being made in the interests of children from that dimly-lit period of the eighteenth century when children's books were just coming to be seen as acceptable products —

[1] One need look no further than the permanent collections on display in the manuscript saloon and in the King's Library at the British Museum. See also the exhaustive discussion of Indian illustration in the catalogue for the exhibition *The Art of the Book in India* (The British Library, 1982).

3 Edward Lear

'How Pleasant to Know Mr Lear!'
Author's holograph ms. of this brief excursion
into autobiography, with a pen and ink sketch,
dated San Remo, 14 January, 1879. The ms. is
accompanied by a letter, written from the
opposite end of the page, disclosing 'a Pome,
which you may or you may knott send to the
Lady who says "How pleasant to know Mr
Lear!"' This was addressed to a Mr Bevan who
was wintering at San Remo with his family. It
is assumed that the 'Lady' was his daughter.

BL. Dept of Manuscripts, Add. Ms. 618918

4 Anon.

'Man's lyfe' and 'Querula Divina' [The Desert
of Religion: a miscellany of English religious
works] Early 15th c.

11 × 18 in. Pen and simple wash.

Two straightforward, unadorned efforts at
representing first the perils of the world and of
Hell, and second the suffering Christ. The
illustration incorporates a medieval 'speech
bubble' with Christ reminding man of His
agonies, and also an emblematic representation
of the Wounded Heart.

BL. Add. Ms. 37049, ff.19b–20

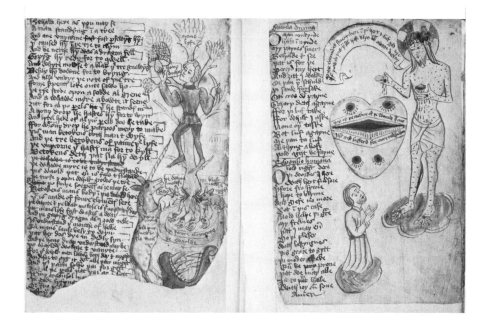

[2] A near facsimile of *Alice's Adventures
Under Ground* was published in 1985, and
this occasioned an exhibition in the British
Library's manuscript saloon which
detailed the making of 'the first *Alice*'.
Thackeray's manuscript of *The Rose and
the Ring* is now in the Pierpont Morgan
Library, New York who (as with Perrault)
published an excellent facsimile of it in
1947. Some eight holograph versions of
The Book of Nonsense exist, possibly made
by Lear for friends or as preparation for
new editions of the book. Most are now
in America and are the subject of an as-
yet unpublished census by Mr Justin G.
Schiller.

one of the earliest and most remarkable of these survivals being the presentation manuscript of Charles Perrault's *Contes de ma Mere Loye* (1695) which
is now in the Pierpont Morgan Library, New York, and was published in
facsimile in 1956. A charming English example is the home-made teaching
apparatus, incorporating spelling and reading exercises, along with a host of
little scrapbook pictures, made by Jane Johnson of Witham Manor for her son
George in the 1740s (Ball Collection; Indiana University).

It is in the nineteenth century however—a time when the picture book
came into its own, and a time which is the main preoccupation of this
handbook—that the home-made picture book abounded. Many amateur
'family' books and magazines can still be found to bear witness to the
Victorians' liking for private book-making (**5**), and the time and care which
many an unassuming household devoted to the exercise is paralleled in the
jeux d'esprit of the more professional. The young Richard Doyle, for instance,
learnt much of his craft in the 'exercises' that he produced for the family circle
(**6**); the mature Walter Crane wrote and illustrated little stories for each of his
children—revealing thereby a freshness and an ease of draughtsmanship that
was often lacking in his published books (**7**). At a yet more distinguished
level one could point to those labours of love that began their existence as
private entertainments and concluded by being classics of the genre. Beyond
all doubt the most famous of these is *Alice's Adventures Under Ground*, the
book that 'Lewis Carroll' wrote out and illustrated for Alice herself. For all the
sentiment attached to it however, it has none of the heart-warming verve of
Thackeray's wonderful manuscript of *The Rose and the Ring*, or of Edward
Lear's numerous drafts and copies of *The Book of Nonsense*.[2].

The freedom and flexibility which the illustrator enjoys in these manuscript books—the opportunity that he gives himself to make a unity of text
and picture—is one of the salient features in the tradition to which Randolph
Caldecott belongs. It is not the only one however, for it is linked to a certain
stance towards the job of illustrating which may never be articulated by the
artist but which may be summed up as Naturalistic.

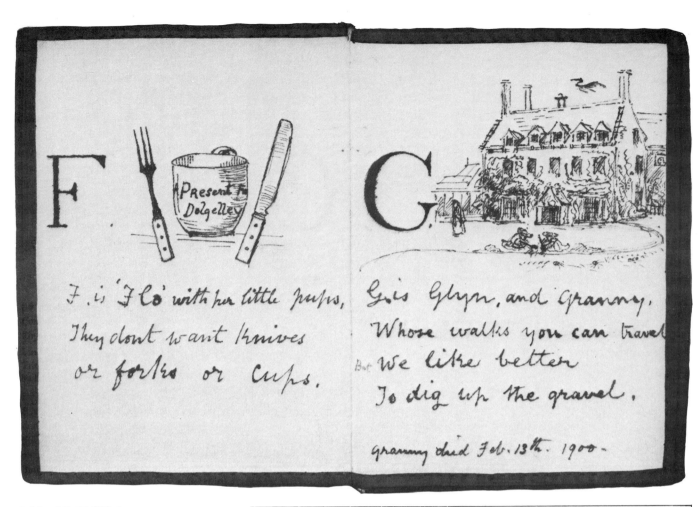

F. is 'Flo' with her little pups,
They dont want knives
or forks or cups.

G. is Glyn, and Granny,
Whose walks you can travel
But We like better
To dig up the gravel.

Granny died Feb. 13th. 1900.

5 L[ucy] E. G[riffiths]

ABC

Glynmalden, 1899. 7½ × 11 in. Pen and ink on linen, the 'leaves' edge-bound in coloured silk and stitched into home-made decorated covers in blue linen.

An alphabet book, hand-written and illustrated by an aunt for her two nephews, referring throughout to events and subjects known to the family. The very amateurishness of the production is testimony to the affection that prompted it.

Private collection, pp.[6–7]

6 Richard Doyle

A Journal kept by Richard Doyle in the Year 1840.

London, Smith, Elder & Co., 1885. 10⅞ × 8¾ in. Photo-litho facsimile of the pen and ink holograph.

The youthful illustrator depicts his delight in the new prints (some of them his own) on display in Fores's shop.

BL. 10855 g 9, p.66

All this week I have been doing a picture of the review on Monday. and of course am very glad when it turned out that Papa likes it. Here fun by the twelve oclock post to day a note arrived directed to Master Dick Doyle. I hastily tore open the document and found it to contain an order from Mr Moore for six Tournaments. I bought them of course. Was ever anything equal to it since the beginning of the world. James came home with an alarm that my thing was in the window of Mrs Fores of Piccadilly. I made off without delay and there to my consternation was the identical culprit lying on its back in the bottom shelf of the window. This certainly is something beyond belief.

Sunday. 31st. Nine oclock Mass. At the show had part of Prince Alberts reviewing the footguards in front of the Horse Guards and Edward VI granting charters.

& intro
=duced to
temporary,
& some
=what lim
=ited quarters
in a biscuit tin.

7 Walter Crane
Mr Michael Mouse Unfolds his Tale ...
reproduced from the original manuscript in the
collection of Mrs Catherine T. Patterson.
Introduction by Mrs Patterson.

New Haven, Yale University Library, 1956. 8 × 6¼ in.
Photo-litho facsimile of the holograph drawing in
pen and ink and water-colour.
BL.x990/1629 p.[4]

For instance, most of the examples of the urge to illustrate given so far are representational: literal portrayals of what the text says. It is of no consequence that the illustrator may in one case be concerned with a 'crazy old Englishman' and in another with the home-comforts of a mouse in a biscuit tin, what matters is that he seeks to give an unadorned account of phenomena as he sees them.

Furthermore, where these events build up into a sequence they tend to be illustrated with a singleness of vision which imposes on them a thematic coherence, whether it coincides with a unitary story or creates a unity out of a disparate jumble of unrelated elements, like the letters of the alphabet, or a series of rhymes or limericks. This homogeneity intensifies the experience of 'reading the pictures', especially where—as, outstandingly, in the books of Caldecott himself—there is a rhythmic progression through the pages, a sense of music and dance', as Maurice Sendak has said.

It is necessary to stress these characteristics early on, even though they appear to be merely the natural and obvious course that any illustrator will take when confronted by the words of his text. For, human nature is not always given to the natural or the obvious, and where the making of illustrations is concerned a variety of influences may occur to modify the degree to which 'literal portrayal' is the dominant mode.

There may be cultural reasons for this. Other societies, affected by different historical or geographical circumstances—or simply by a difference in the materials available for writing or drawing—may adopt a pictorial language that converts plain representationalism into forms that are stylised almost to abstraction. It is impossible here to generalise about how far such stylisation finds its way into processes that might be seen as illustrative,[3] although our modern eclecticism has not ruled out Western experimentation with them. The quest by picture-book artists for graphic originality, or for 'ethnic roots', has brought exotic styles into the nursery (**8**, **9**).

One does not need to go too far from home however to find alternative methods for conjoining text and picture in a way which neglects or disrupts the balance between the two. From its very beginnings, for instance, the British manuscript tradition was wedded to an illustrative mode that was decorative rather than representational. Whether one thinks of the elaborate designs built into the lettering of Celtic manuscripts, or of the filigree painting in the illuminations of later devotional works, one is contemplating an attitude towards illustration which sees the content of pictures as subordinate to their place in the design of the page (**10**).

Such an approach, with its emphasis on technical skills of a high order, has proved seductive to artists and audience alike, but its application to picture books has often been inimical to the integrity of the book as a means of communication rather than just 'a physical product'. The force of a text may be diluted or even lost, behind artistic bravura; the mind ceases to attend to narrative implications in the appreciation of visual distractions or cleverness (**11**, **12**).

A somewhat similar critical issue is raised by the intrusion of what might be called painterly effects into the ideally fluid progress of the picture book. Here though we are less concerned with a narrative content in the picture that is subordinate to a decorative pattern than with a pictorial representation that takes precedence over the text through the spaciousness, the drama, the detail of its execution (**13**, **14**, **15**). (While it is true that in both decorative and painterly illustration one may often be dealing with books whose texts have a clumsiness or a triviality that is only redeemed by the glamour of the pictures, this is hardly an argument in favour of such illustrative methods in themselves.)

One further example of picture books that are liable to place a disproportionate emphasis on pictorial features is that of the emblem and the rebus books. Indeed, in so far as the pictorial idea precedes that of its verbalisation such books are almost bound to depend for their life on the illustrator's contribution. Historically speaking, they are of considerable interest, since their moral or religious message may have made them approved reading for children at a time when few other amusing picture books, apart from Aesop's *Fables*, were likely to come their way (**16**, **17**, **18**). Nevertheless their later manifestations—as books for playing games with rather than as coherent self-sufficient imaginative experiences—put them beyond any serious

8 Fiona French
Huni
London, Oxford University Press, 1971. $11\frac{1}{4} \times 17$ in. Photo-litho reproduction of a drawing in line and water-colour.

An attempt to illustrate an Egyptian legend in the style of an Egyptian painting. The flat diagrammatic treatment of events demands a degree of visual attention which holds up the even progress of the story.
BL. x992/1054, pp.[8–9]

[3] The fortunate circumstance of the exhibition being held within a few feet of the King's Library means that visitors could have immediate access to a wide variety of examples of illustrative styles from other cultures.

9 Gerald McDermott
Anansi the Spider; a tale from Ashanti
London, Hamish Hamilton, 1973. 8×18 in. Photo-litho reproduction of a painting in acrylic ink.

An attempt to adapt Ashanti art to the re-telling of an Ashanti folktale. The static patterning is given a hint of movement by the depiction of a sequence of events on one page-opening, and by a dynamic use of typography. The resources of such a graphic style are, however, severely limited.
BL. x998/3263, pp.[10–11]

One time Anansi went a long way from home. Far from home. He got lost. He fell into trouble.

consideration as contributing to the art of the picture book (**19**).

As seen here, that art is essentially one of sobriety and coherence. It does not preclude linguistic or pictorial high jinks, but it does ask that the two modes of expression work alongside and enhance each other. Technical or graphic wizardry will always appeal to the journalist instinct, ever on the look-out for eye-catching excitements, but the artistry celebrated in the following pages—whether by Caldecott or Cruikshank, Bennett or Burningham—achieves its status through simple drawing and by underplaying rather than emphasising pictorial effects.

No burial this pretty pair
Of any man receives,
Till Robin-red-breast piously
Did cover them with leaves.

And now the heavy wrath of God
Upon their uncle fell;
Yea, fearful fiends did haunt his
house,
His conscience felt an hell:

His barns were fir'd, his goods
consum'd,
His lands were barren made,
His cattle died within the field,
And nothing with him stayd.

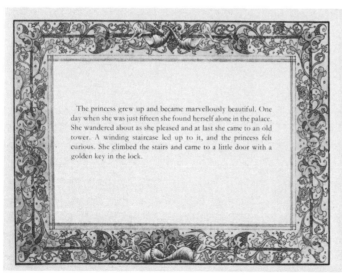

The princess grew up and became marvellously beautiful. One day when she was just fifteen she found herself alone in the palace. She wandered about as she pleased and at last she came to an old tower. A winding staircase led up to it, and the princess felt curious. She climbed the stairs and came to a little door with a golden key in the lock.

10 [An English Psalter]

*c.*1220. Illuminated manuscript.

Historiated initial letter 'B' from the Beatus page, the letter itself almost submerged beneath designs prompted by the theme that it introduces.

BL. Cotton Ms. Vespasian A. i. f.lv

11 Anon.

The Babes in the Wood

London, Sampson Low, Son & Co, 1861. 7¼ × 5¼ in. A water-colour (?) original 'printed in colours by W. Dickes'. A complex job with litho tints overlaid with an engraved metal key-plate and the colours probably added from relief-metal plates.

Victorian medievalism decorating a late medieval ballad. Compare the sentimentality of the design with the brusqué woodcuts of nos. **21**, **22** (below) and with the touching but un-serious narrative treatments by Caldecott and by Ardizzone (**93**).

BL. 1347 f 10, f.[9]

12 The Brothers Grimm

Thorn Rose; illustrated by Errol Le Cain

London, Faber & Faber, 1975. 7⅜ × 19¼ in. Photo-litho reproduction of a water-colour drawing.

Modern medievalism applied to a traditional tale. The unadorned, not to say flat, text has become an excuse for decorative virtuosity.

BL. Cup 1281/55, pp.[12–13]

13 Anon.

The Elegant Girl; or virtuous principles the true source of elegant manners; illustrated by twelve drawings with lines to each, and a poem called The Mother

London, S. Inman, 1817. 9 × 14½ in. Hand-coloured stipple engraving.

The picture selected here is neither the most elaborate nor the most colourful in this luxurious picture book (whose original price was 16s., which might be interpreted as well over £200 today). It does however show that the pursuit of elegance through virtue may result in the abandonment of vitality.

BL. c 175 b 44 Plate 10

14 Carové [F.W.]

The Story Without an End, trans. from the German by Sarah Austin. With illustrations printed in colour after drawings by E[leanor] V[ere] B[oyle].

London, Sampson Low, Son and Marston, 1868 Image size 6½ × 4⅛ in. Printed in oil colours, probably from wood blocks, by Leighton Bros.

It is hard not to see an influence from Blake in Lady Boyle's water-colours for Carové's pseudo-mystical vapourings, but the wiry line has got lost behind the un-co-ordinated images.

13

14

HEY diddle diddle, the cat and the fiddle,
The cow jumped over the moon;
The little dog laughed
To see such sport,
And the dish ran away with the spoon.

15 Trad.

Nicola Bayley's Book of Nursery Rhymes.

London, Jonathan Cape, 1975. 9⅝ × 14¼ in. Photo-litho reproduction of a water-colour drawing.

A composite picture, finished in every detail, but failing to reflect the lively activity of the rhyme. Compare the naïvete of the child's drawing (**1**, above) or the epic interpretation by Caldecott.
BL. 990/7158 pp.[27–8]

16 George Wither

A Collection of Emblemes, Ancient and Moderne . . . The fourth booke.

London, printed by Augustine Mathewes, 1634. 12 × 8½ in. Emblems engraved by the Dutchman Crispin van de Passe; letterpress text.
BL. c 70 h 5 p.225

Although the idea for the picture could have come from one of the tales of the Wise Men of Gotham, it has been turned to long-winded moral purposes. The book was not intended for children but it found its way to a broad popular market through: —

17 R[obert] B[urton] (i.e. Nathaniel Crouch)

Delights for the Ingenious in above fifty select and choice emblems; curiously engraven on copper plates.
Collected by R.B. for Nath. Crouch at the Bell, the Poultry, near Cheapside, 1684. 6 × 4 in. Engraved illustrations, letterpress text.

A plagiarism of Wither by a publisher who specialised in popular adaptations and whose books were commended by Samuel Johnson for 'reluctant readers'. The 'curiously engraven plates' have reversed (and greatly simplified) the original prints.
BL. G 13220, pp.50–51

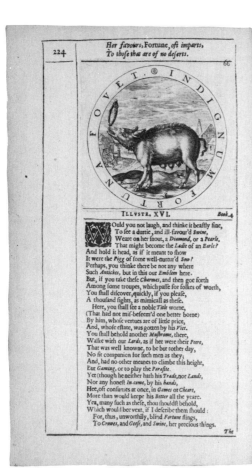

ILLVSTR. XVI.   Book.4.

WOuld you not laugh, and thinke it beastly fine,
To see a durtie, and ill-favour'd *Swine*,
Weare on her snout, a *Diamond*, or a *Pearle*,
That might become the *Ladie* of an *Earle*?
And hold it head, as if it meant to show
It were the *Pigg* of some well-nurtur'd *Soo*?
Perhaps, you thinke there be not any where
Such *Antickes*, but in this our *Emblem* here.
But, if you take these *Charmes*, and then goe forth
Among some troupes, which passe for folkes of worth,
You shall discover, quickly, if you please,
A thousand sights, as mimicall as these.
Here, you shall see a noble *Title* worne,
(That had not mis-beseem'd one better borne)
By him, whose vertues are of little price,
And, whose estate, was gotten by his *Vice*.
You shall behold another *Mushrome*, there,
Walke with our *Lords*, as if hee were their *Peere*,
That was well knowne, to be but tother day,
No fit companion for such men as they;
And, had no other meanes to climbe this height,
But *Gaming*, or to play the *Parasite*.
Yet (though he neither hath his *Trade*, nor *Lands*,
Nor any honest *In-come*, by his *hands*,
Hee, oft consumes at once, in *Games* or *Cheats*,
More than would keepe his *Better* all the yeare.
Yea, many such as these, thou shouldst behold,
Which would bee vext, if I describe them should:
For, thus, unworthily, blind *Fortune* flings,
To *Crowes*, and *Geese*, and *Swine*, her precious things.

The

The best good-turnes that Fooles can doe us,
Proove disadvantages unto us.
225
67

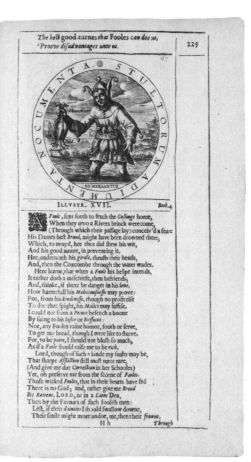

NE MERGANTVR

ILLVSTR. XVII.   Book.4.

A *Foole*, sent forth to fetch the *Goslings* home,
When they unto a Rivers brinck were come,
(Through which their passage lay) conceiv'd a feare
His Dames best *Brood*, might have been drowned there,
Which, to avoyd, hee thus did shew his wit,
And his good nature, in preventing it.
Hee, underneath his *girdle*, thrusts their heads,
And, then the Coxcombe through the water wades.
Here learne, that when a *Foole* his helpe intends,
It rather doth a mischiefe, then befriends;
And, thinke, if there be danger in his *love*,
How harmfull his *Maliciousnesse* may prove:
For, from his *kindnesse*, though no profit rise
To doe thee spight, his *Malice* may suffise.
I could not from a *Prince* beseech a boone
By suing to his *Jester* or *Buffoone*:
Nor, any Fooles vaine humor, sooth or serve,
To get my bread, though I were like to starve.
For, to be *poore*, I should not blush so much,
As if a *Foole* should raise me to be *rich*.
Lord, though of such a kinde my faults may be,
That sharpe *Affliction* still must tutor mee,
(And give me due *Correction* in her Schooles)
Yet, oh preserve me from the scorne of *Fooles*,
Those wicked *Fooles*, that in their hearts have sed
There is no God; and, rather give me *Bread*
By *Ravens*, LORD, or in a *Lions* Den,
Then by the Favours of such foolish men:
Lest, if their *dainties* I should swallow downe,
Their smile might more undoe, me, then their frowne.

H h   Through

16

Emblem XIII.

Emb: 13.

Stultorum *Adjumenta* Nocumenta.

Th

THE
Thirteenth Emblem
Illustrated.

*The best good turns that Fools can do us.
Prove disadvantages unto us.*

A Fool, sent forth to fetch the *Goslings* home,
When they unto a Rivers brink were come,
(Through which their passage lay) conceiv'd a
                                            (fear,
His Dames best *Brood* might have been drown'd
                                            (there ;
Which, to avoid, he thus did shew his wit,
And his good nature, in preventing it.
He, underneath his *girdle*, thrusts their heads,
And then the Coxcomb through the water wades.

D 2   Here

17

23

18 [Cat]herine Sinclair

A [Sun]day [Letter]

Edinburgh, James Wood etc., 1863. $8\frac{3}{4} \times 5\frac{3}{4}$ in. Lithographed.

Rebus books became popular in the eighteenth century when 'hieroglyphic Bibles' were seen as an enjoyable way of imparting a knowledge of the scriptures. Here the author Catherine Sinclair (who wrote the famous children's story *Holiday House*) adapts the idea in one of several hieroglyphic letters. She uses pictures both to denote objects and to represent syllables.

BL. 012804 h13, p[5]

19 Kit Williams

Masquerade

London, Jonathan Cape, 1979. $10\frac{7}{8} \times 8\frac{3}{8}$ in. Photo-litho reproduction of mixed-media paintings.

The most contorted riddle-book ever. It became a bestseller because of the puzzle that it set and not because it possessed in any way the visual and narrative integrity that are the qualities of a successful picture book. The riddle solved, it has had nothing more to offer (except a deeply unsatisfactory sequel).

BL. x992/3818, p.[7]

AND THE SLEEPY HOURS OF NIGHT THE DAY BEGINS ARE OVER

Representational illustration and illustrative techniques

Woodcuts

The use of illustrations to give a literal, unadorned interpretation of the events of a text commended itself strongly to the first printers. It may have been something of a revelation to them to realise that, as well as having the capacity to reproduce texts more or less indefinitely, they could also reproduce images[4]; when called upon to fashion these images however they saw no reason to go beyond a descriptive brief, which, they probably argued—cogently enough—was what the public expected. When Chaucer writes of the Wife of Bath then Caxton assumes that readers of his printed edition of the *Canterbury Tales* would like to know what she looks like and gets his wood-cutter to supply a picture; if the scene needs setting for a lesson in 'logyke' then what better than a master reading to his pupils (**20**)—even if the result, which is among the earliest illustrations ever to be printed in England, turns out to be 'one of the poorest cuts ever inserted between covers' (Edward Hodnett, *English Woodcuts 1480–1535*. Oxford, 1973, p.1.)

Woodcutting as a reproductive method may have been in its infancy just then, but it has always been a forceful, direct—not to say rough and ready—craft, which is willing to leave plenty to the reader's imagination. It is among the simplest of the graphic processes, working on the principle that a block of wood, standing the same height as type-metal, can be used to print an outline drawing at the same time as the accompanying text. The drawing, and whatever simple shading is required, can be made on the surface of the block (always bearing in mind that it will print a mirror-impression, reversing all the features and any lettering that may appear). Redundant wood is then cut from the surface with a knife, so that the lines and shading, standing proud, are ready to print. The cutting is usually done on the lateral- or plank-grain of the wood, and although this is subject to hazards of temperature or damp, so that splitting or warping may occur, and although the grubby bustle of a print-shop may lead to surface damage, the hardihood of woodcut blocks is quite remarkable. Many survived not only long print-runs but also promiscuous transference from one text to another, provided some very general

[4] For a study of the psychological and social impact of picture-reproduction and its relation to available processes see William Ivins Jr.'s pioneering *Prints and Visual Communication* (London, 1953).

20 Anon.
The Myrrour of the World
Woodcuts.

The sheer badness of the craftsmanship here helps to give an insight into the skill required to elicit convincing pictures from the surface of a wooden block.

BL. c 10 b 5, p.20v

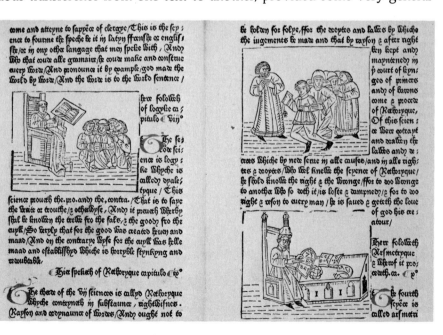

21 Anon.

The History of the Two Children in the Wood
Newcastle upon Tyne, J. White, n.d. [1710?].
6½ × 4½ in. Woodcut.
BL 12612 b 15(2) cover

There is a near-medieval roughness about the cutting of this block for a chapbook cover (designed to attract custom). The composition has a certain sophistication about it, however, for it shows in one frame a selection of events from the story, even down to the rogues' hanging.

This was a customary ploy, especially with this tale, as may be seen from the following London edition:-

22 Anon.

The History of the Two Children in the Wood
London, printed by and for W.O. and sold by the Booksellers n.d. [1720?]. 6 × 7 in. Woodcut.
BL. 12612 d 8, cover

relevance was present.

These cheap, simple, unambitious cuts were a staple in popular books during the eighteenth century when trade in children's books was beginning to develop. Traditional stories like *Guy of Warwick* or *The Children in the Wood* (**21**, **22**) were hawked about fairs and markets by the chapmen or 'running stationers' and were probably read by old and young alike; by the middle of the century chapbooks clearly intended primarily for children were also to be found (**23**). The brevity of such books, and of the early alphabet books (so easily fitted into a standard sixteen or thirty-two page format), make them the forerunners of the picture book as we know it (**24**)—and it is worth noting that several of the titles that Caldecott called upon in his 'Toy Book' series were originally bestsellers among the chapbook merchants.

Woodcutting was later to give way to the finer craft of wood-engraving, but it, or the draughtsmanship that it encouraged, has been called upon in books where broad or chunky illustrations seemed suitable. There was a conscious revival of the style made by the Newcastle businessman/woodcutter/and self-styled loafer, Joseph Crawhall, who produced a dozen or so books in which eccentrically comic texts were perfectly matched with chapbook-style 'sculptures'. In his turn he influenced the Beggarstaff Brothers (James Pryde and William Nicholson) in their poster-making at the end of the nineteenth century and Nicholson cut, rather than engraved, woodblocks for his *Alphabet* of 1899, the forerunner of his other large illustrated albums. In modern times some picture-book artists, like Marcia Brown in America and Edward Bawden in England, have cut their original illustrations on wood (or in lino—which gives a closely related effect) and these have then been converted into plates suitable for high-speed, long-run printing.

Engravings on metal

The simplicity of the stories and rhymes in the nursery books of the eighteenth century is aptly reflected in their almost diagrammatic woodcuts—

THE HOUSE THAT JACK Built.

A diverting Story for CHILDREN of all Ages.

Sold at the Printing Office Aldermsy Church-yard.

This is the House that JACK built.

This is the Malt — that lay in the House — that Jack built.

This is the Rat — that eat the Malt — that lay in the House — that Jack built.

This is the Cat — that kill'd the Rat — that eat the Malt — that Lay the House — that Jack built:

This is the Dog — that worried the Cat that kill'd the Rat — that eat the Malt—that lay in the House— that Jack built.

This is the Cow with the crumpled Horn—that tossed the Dog — that worried the Cat — that kill'd the Rat — that eat the Malt — that lay in the House that Jack built.

This is the Maiden all forlorn——that milked the Cow with the crumpled Horn — that tossed the Dog — that worried the Cat — hat kill'd the Rat—that eat the Malt — that lay in the House that Jack built.

This is the Man all tatter'd and torn — that kissed the Maiden all forlorn—that milked the Cow with the crumpled Horn — that tossed the Dog—that worried the Cat— that killed the Rat — that eat the Malt — that lay in the House that Jack built.

This is the Priest all shaven and shorn — that married the Man all tatter'd and torn — that kissed the Maiden all forlorn — that milked the Cow with the crumpled Horn—that tossed the Dog—that worried the Cat —that killed the Rat —that eat the Malt—that lay in the House that Jack built.

This is the Cock that crow'd 'n the Morn---that waked the Priest all shaven and shorn--- that marry'd the Man all tatter'd and torn---that kissed the Maiden all forlorn---that mil-

ked the Cow with the crumpled Horn --- that tossed the Dog---that worry'd the Cat--- that killed the Rat--- that eat the Malt — that lay in the House that Jack built.

24 Anon.

A New Lottery Book of Birds and Beasts for Children to Learn their Letters by as Soon as They Can Speak

Newcastle, printed by T. Saint for W. Charnley, 1771. 4 × 5½ in. Typographic fleurons and woodcuts.

One of the books printed by Saint on which Thomas Bewick worked in his 'prentice years. The matching of word and image is carried out unpretentiously, as was the custom in these little books, but already something of Bewick's delicate touch can be seen. (A bovine solution has been found to the perennial problem in alphabet books of finding words and pictures for the intractable 'X'.)

BL. ch 770/16, pp.[46–47]

23 Trad.

The House that Jack Built. A diverting story for children of all ages

London, sold at the Printing Office Aldermary Church-yard, n.d. [c.1770]. Page size approx. 3¾ × 2¼ in. Woodcuts.

One of the earliest known printed versions of the nursery rigmarole that was chosen by Randolph Caldecott as the subject of his first venture into picture-book-making. The British Library copy of this chapbook is in unfolded state (i.e. not yet folded into a 16-page booklet ready for sale). In this illustration 12 pages have been photographed in sequence to show the progress of the story and the wood-cutter's gallant attempt at a fully representational interpretation.

BL. 11621 e 4(24), pp.[1]–12

aides-memoires almost, fitting into no clearly defined background scene (**25**). For those publishers who sought a more elaborate visual representation however there was always the resource of illustrative printing from incised metal-plates.

Copper-engraving or etching or some mixture of the two has a history not much shorter than that of woodcutting, but is a craft that has been more applicable to the market for pictures and prints than for illustrated books. The essential feature of the technique is that the artist causes the lines and shading of his drawing to be cut into the surface of a copper plate, either directly with engraving tools or more gradually by working with a needle on an acid-resistant covering to the plate, so that acid will etch out the lines to varying depths. When the plate is ready (and its preparation may be complicated by a variety of more sophisticated techniques such as mezzotinting or aquatinting) it is covered with a layer of ink. This is then wiped off, so that ink only remains in the incised lines, and the picture is printed by running plate and paper through a high pressure rolling-press, rather like a mangle.

The virtue of plate-printing as a process is first the degree of detail that it permits the artist to achieve and second the extent to which he may remain in control of the final image, so that it is not surprising to find that The Print in the hands of a Rembrandt, a Goya or a Palmer, can attain effects as powerful as anything in the arts of painting or drawing. As a medium for book illustration however the process has several disadvantages. The gain in precision and control is offset first by the need to ink, wipe and print each impression of the plate as a separate operation, second by the need to do this on a different press from the one on which letterpress is printed, third (and consequent upon this) by the frequent requirement to print plates on separate sheets of paper, often of different stock, which must be inserted into the

26 [Thomas Rowlandson]

Copper-plate printers at work [n.d.]
Reproduced from A. Hind, *A History of Engraving and Etching* (Reprinted, New York, 1963), p.236.

Etching the etchers. An informal, hastily-made plate, perhaps executed by Rowlandson as a 'Sketch' while he was in the print-shop.

25 Anon.

A Little Pretty Pocket-book for the Instruction and Amusement of Little Master Tommy and Pretty Miss Polly ... the tenth edition

London, printed for John Newbery ..., 1760.
4 × 7 in. Woodcuts.

First published in 1744, this compendium of rhymes-with-morals, nursery rhymes, fables etc. made extensive use of woodcuts. Their plain representationalism was not very skilled, but at least had a nice congruence with the laboured text. The huntsman in quest of his game, however, and the dancing cat (shown here) are at the start of a tradition that will lead to Caldecott's *The Three Jovial Huntsmen* and *Hey Diddle Diddle*.

BL. ch 760/6. Sigs. D3r

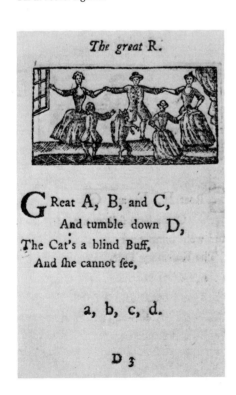

sequence of letterpress sheets, and fourth by the fact that copper is a soft metal which wears quickly, so that many fewer impressions of a picture may be printed than from the resilient surface of a wood-block.

The cost in time, labour and materials that is incurred by the use of copper plates for illustrated books has tended severely to restrict their appearance in children's books, whose lack of significance (for adults) has helped to ensure that they be cheaply produced and speedily disposed of. The fine etchings that Francis Barlow—first English master of the craft—supplied for editions of Aesop's *Fables* (**27**) were a prestige job, by no means intended for the schoolroom (even though they found their way there), and much of the plate-work in eighteenth-century children's books was found in single examples, such as frontispieces,[5] or in expensively-conceived books where the print-run was unlikely to be regularly repeated.

There was one way however in which plate-making could be made more economical and that was by running editions of books entirely from metal plates without the awkward combination with letterpress printing. This naturally meant that any text that was present with the pictures would also have to be engraved, but—so far as the aesthetics of the matter are concerned—this could be an advantage since it could restore a balance and a homogeneity to the appearance of the page. The magical *Tommy Thumb's Pretty Song Book* of c.1744 (on permanent display in the King's Library) is a curious early example of the process applied to what seems to be the first ever book of popular nursery rhymes.

[5] As evidence of the transitory nature of copper as a printing surface one may still discover the way in which its intaglio images deteriorate in children's books that proved perhaps more popular than expected. The *Orbis Pictus* by Amos Comenius—a remarkable pictorial encyclopaedia, that also served as a manual for teaching Latin—had its illustrations printed from copper-plates in the first English edition of 1659. These can be seen thinning out and giving poor impressions in the later editions. And in T. Carnan's edition of 'Tommy Trapwit's' *Be Merry and Wise*, 1781, the original engraved frontispiece used in the early 1750s has worn out and has been replaced by a much inferior woodcut.

By far the most important consequences of the use of plate-printing in the making of complete children's books occurred at the beginning of the nineteenth century, when the picture book as we understand it today sprang fully-bedizened from the rolling-press in a variety of styles that bear witness to the possibilities of the process (see below). But there was one unusual phenomenon that preceded it—which may be seen not so much as the precursor of picture books as of pop-ups.

This was the harlequinade, or turn-up book, which put in an appearance as a significant component of the eighteenth century book-trade at the end of the 1760s. It was constructed as follows: a lower leaf was printed from a single engraved plate with its text and pictures divided into eight panels, four along the top and four along the bottom. Hinged to the long upper and lower edges of this sheet there was a second leaf, printed in similar divisions but this time cut lengthwise along the middle and upright-wise between the two sets of four panels. Such cutting made eight hinged flaps of the upper sheet so that as the 'book' was 'read', one turned up, or turned down flap after flap and obtained a series of gradually changing images which followed the 'story' (usually written in a set of six-line stanzas). By folding the sheets into four along the vertical alignment the 'book' took on something of the appearance of a modern slim-line diary.

The idea for these harlequinades seems to have arrived a hundred years earlier in a moral work composed from woodcuts (28). Their period of popularity was due largely to the exploitation of the dodge by the publisher Robert Sayer, whose work was fairly quickly imitated by the firm of William Tringham and by other booksellers. Many of the themes for the turn-ups were based upon theatrical scenes that relate tangentially to the tradition of *commedia del'arte*—hence the name 'harlequinade' and hence the inapplicability of much of the subject-matter to the affairs of childhood. Nevertheless, some turn-ups did make reference to themes with which children would be familiar (29)—and one remarkable example related to Hogarth is noted below. The principle of their operation is today found almost exclusively in the comic movables, known generically as 'heads, bodies and legs' books (30), for which manuscript precedents go back at least to the early nineteenth century.

The making of picture books from copper—and later, steel—plates has only a desultory history beyond the first twenty years of the nineteenth century. With the coming of photographic processes for the reproduction of line drawings, engraving could do little that was not as easily attainable with pen and ink. When artists have turned to plate-making it has usually been because of the challenge of experimenting with the effects that can be gained from 'the bite of the print', or for the making of illustrations for prestige works which (in original form) have never got near the nursery.

Relief metal engravings

Given the use of metal for intaglio printing, one might reasonably ask why metal surfaces might not also be used to print illustrations in much the same way as woodblocks. As it happens, some activity in the eighteenth century was devoted to this end, but (with one astonishing maverick example dealt with on p. 46 below) printing from relief metal was never widely practised.

27 Aesop

Aesop's Fables with his Life: in English, French and Latin ... illustrated with one hundred and twelve sculptures ... by Francis Barlow

London, printed by William Godbid for Francis Barlow ... 1666. Plate size 6¼ × 6¼ in. Etching on copper.

Perhaps the first great example of narrative illustration to appear from an English artist. Barlow's etchings are masterly both for the way they portray animals and for the scene-setting that gives 'a local habitation and a name' to the Aesopic stories (observe the huntsman riding to apprehend the captured lion). Barlow's images in this fable sequence have been copied in editions published for children almost down to the present time.

BL. c 70 h3, p.47

The best-known example is probably that of the *Fables* of Aesop, didactically edited by Samuel Croxall, and furnished with soft-metal relief engravings by Elisha Kirkall.

These relief engravings exhibit nuances of detail beyond anything that was possible in the woodcutting of the period and, insofar as they draw upon Francis Barlow's earlier designs for Aesop's *Fables*, they mark a transitional stage between the original etching of images and their appearance as wood-engravings (see below, p. 35). Evidence from the long sequence of printings in which cuts were used, however, shows clearly that the metal surface did not take kindly to heavy use and it is probable that publishers did not see enough advantage in the technique to use it widely as an alternative to the simpler and longer-lasting woodcuts. Where it did find a brief but happy future was among the colour printers of the mid-nineteenth century, some of whom chose relief metal rather than wood for building up a sequence of colour tints on an original outline print.

Wood engravings

The momentous change in the quality of image that could be achieved with relief printing came with the refinement of wood-cutting techniques into

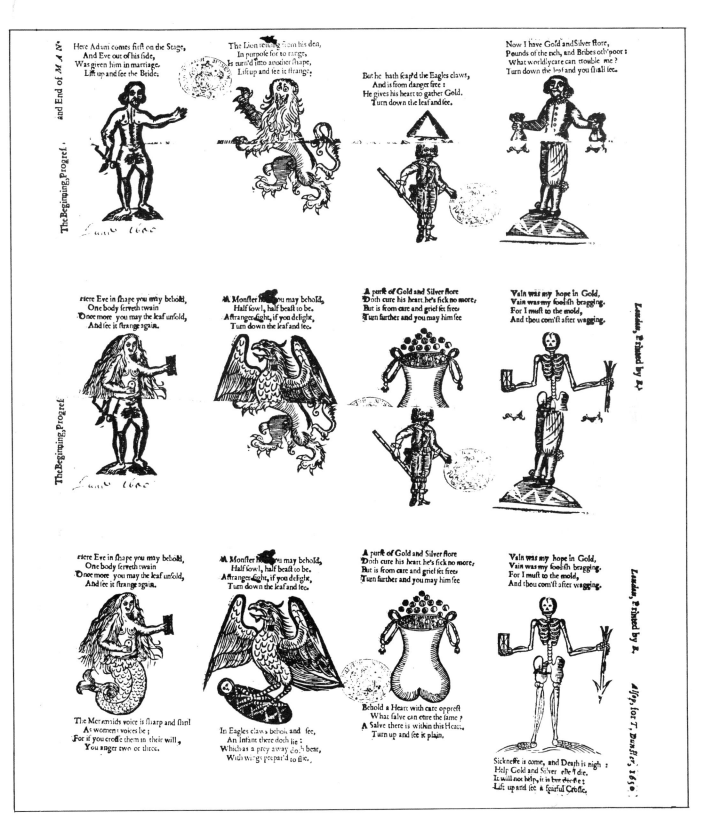

28 Anon.

The Beginning, Progress and End of Man

London, printed by B. Alsop, for T. Dunster, 1650. 9 × 4 in. Woodcuts.

Parent of the eighteenth-century turn-ups or harlequinades, seen here in various pictorial states as
the flaps are raised.

BL. 669 f 15 (34). Single sheet

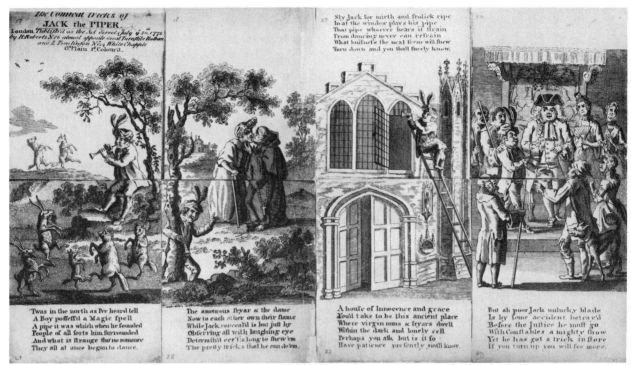

The Comical Tricks of
JACK the PIPER.
London Publish'd as the Act directs July y 30. 1772
by H.Roberts N.16 almost opposite Great Turnstile Holborn
and L. Tomlinson N.14 White Chappell
6.ᵈ Plain 1.ˢ Colour'd.

Sly Jack for mirth and frolick ripe
In at the window plays his pipe
That pipe whoever hears it strain
From dancing never can refrain
What buisness the next Scene will shew
Turn down and you shall surely know.

'Twas in the north as I've heard tell
A Boy possess'd a Magic spell
A pipe it was which when he sounded
People of all sorts him surrounded
And what is strange tho' no romance
They all at once began to dance.

The amorous fryar & the dame
Now to each other own their flame
While Jack conceal'd is but just by
Observing all with laughing eye
Determin'd eer 'tis long to shew 'em
The pretty tricks that he can do 'em.

A house of Innocence and grace
You'd take to be this ancient place
Where virgin nuns & fryars dwell
Within the dark and lonely cell
Perhaps you ask but is it so
Have patience presently you'll know

But ah poor Jack unlucky blade
Is by some accident betray'd
Before the Justice he must go
With Constables a mighty shew
Yet he has got a trick in store
If you turn up you will see more.

29 Anon.

The Comical Tricks of Jack the Piper

London, H. Roberts … July 30, 1772. 7 × 12½ in. Engraved throughout.

The fashion for 'turn-ups' or 'harlequinades' was started by the publisher Robert Sayer, and H. Roberts seems to have been a competitor and/or a collaborator. This specimen of his work suggests an influence from 'Tom, Tom, the Piper's Son', but it is not certain that children would follow all the merriment over scandal and lechery. (An example of later harlequinades intended for children is given below: **42**.)

BL. C135 f 19(2)

30 Denis Wirth-Miller and Richard Chopping

Heads Bodies & Legs

Harmondsworth, A Puffin Picture Book, 1946. 6 × 8½ in. Photo-litho reproduction of colour-separated drawings.

A familiar modern use of the flap-device that originated with the turn-up books. This is a do-it-yourself version. When the reader has cut the pages into three sections these can be individually turned to make pictures of fantastic creatures. The illustrator Richard Chopping worked on a number of early Puffins, but later achieved fame as the creator of the *coup l'oeil* dust-jackets for the 'James Bond' books.

Private collection. Centre spread

what is generally known as wood engraving. This change involved the use of hard, close-grained woods (usually box) which were worked not on the lateral- or plank-grain but on the much more resilient end-grain. This presented to the engraver a surface which could be worked over in great detail with a variety of cutting tools and which could produce printing surfaces that had all the strength and adaptability of woodcuts (long print runs, with letterpress text and block being printed simultaneously) and would take much of the illustrative detail, albeit within a more restricted area, that had hitherto only been possible on metal plates.

The potential of this mode of illustration—and, indeed, some of the finest examples of its use—is seen in the work of the Newcastle craftsman, Thomas Bewick. His natural ability as a maker of illustrations is already apparent in prentice cuts that he made in 1776 under the influence of the Barlow-Kirkall fable illustrations (**31**), a sequence to which he returned in full-dress dignity in 1818, but the first great demonstration of his use of wood engraving as a technique was in 'educational' works: the *History of Quadrupeds* of 1790 and the two volumes of the *History of Birds* published in 1797 and 1804.

These books can hardly be regarded as picture books, even though they were heavily illustrated and included children among their intended readership. They are significant for the picture-book tradition however because of Thomas Bewick's attractive habit of incorporating into them what he called 'tale pieces'. Appearing usually (as might be expected) at the ends of the various descriptions of animals and birds, these 'tale pieces' had only slight reference to the descriptive leanings of the text but formed instead a quite separate visual commentary depicting scenes and incidents of contemporary—usually rural—life. What Bewick brought to these little engravings was a narrative rather than a descriptive touch. Within the small compass of his block he would give the reader a visual story, to be interpreted as the reader chose (**32**).

As 'tales', therefore, these 'pieces' demonstrate narrative illustration at work in a way which is independent of, even if it complements, the text. They are harbingers of the power that illustrators took unto themselves to imagine scenes or events that are congruent with but may not be directly called for by their subjects. The introduction of such a pictorial commentary was one of the features of Randolph Caldecott's contribution to picture-book art, and he shares too with Bewick not just a natural graphic skill but also a delight in summoning up in his drawings the atmosphere and the character of the people and animals who inhabit the English countryside.

The potential of wood engraving as a graphic process, so ably demonstrated by Thomas Bewick (and indeed also by his brother John, who did much journeyman-work for children's books, but died an early death) was not lost on the publishers of the increasingly book-conscious nineteenth century. Bewick himself trained a school of followers and the division of labour which he may have introduced—with a master perhaps putting designs on the blocks and later 'finishing' them, while pupils or apprentices undertook the intermediate work—came to be applied in a more thoroughgoing manner as the demand for book and magazine illustrations increased. It led to the formation of the classic engraving houses such as those of the Dalziel Brothers in 1840 and, in 1851, of Edmund Evans—the man responsible for

31 Aesop

Select Fables in Three Parts . . . a new edition improved

Newcastle, printed by and for T. Saint, 1784. Block size 1¾ × 2⁵⁄₁₆ in. Wood engravings (reproduced here from a nineteenth-century facsimile reprint).

Bewick first cut this block for an edition of the *Fables* that was published in 1776 soon after he had come out of his apprenticeship. In 1784, in a sharper, possibly re-touched, version it forms part of an extended series of more sophisticated engravings in which his control of detail has been fully mastered. The pictorial theme of the cut was a common one in fable and emblem books of the eighteenth-century, and was to receive a startlingly new interpretation from another hand (**40** below).

commissioning the Toy Book series from Randolph Caldecott.[6]

At first the representation of original art work through the engraved block was done entirely manually. It might be (as frequently occurred with Bewick's designs) that the drawing was traced, in reverse, on the surface of the block and the details worked up from that; or it might be (as occurred with much work in mid-century) that the artist drew his design directly on the block, trusting—not always with confidence—that the engraver would do justice to it thus. In fact, engravers often allowed themselves a good deal of latitude in their interpretations and the final printed pictures may be seen as collaborations rather than the work of an illustrator only.

With the development of photographic emulsions it became possible so to treat the surface of the wood that a drawing could be transferred to it by the action of light, with the result that an artist could make his drawing on paper (which would be preserved) and at the same time ensure that a faithful image would confront the engraver. By this time it had also become possible to reproduce large drawings by slotting or bolting a group of rectangular blocks together, and various methods had been devised for printing in colour from wood-block surfaces.

All-in-all therefore, the development of wood engraving greatly increased the potential of the illustrator. It is true that he could not be in final control of

---

[6] A charming description of this division of labour is given by Caldecott himself in a letter to Juliana Horatia Ewing on 18 October 1883. He writes: 'You ask me the question "Is it true that E.E. is not an engraver?" I thought you knew something of how the "wood engravers" manage their affairs. I will try to explain a little. E.E. has learnt thoroughly his profession and worked at it closely, and as artistically as is usual in this century, for many years (so I believe). But as it is impossible to make any money by sticking to the bench and graver and trying to engrave each block which he engages to do with his own hand, he has called in the assistance of sundry youths whom he has educated in his own style, and when they have become accomplished engravers he has endeared them to him by means of regular weekly payments of money. And in course of time he has felt so satisfied with their ability that he has been content to superintend their work and to give advice and make suggestions thereon at such moments as he could spare from his growing occupations of waiting in publishers' lobbies, of corresponding with authors, of seeking out suitable materials to his trade, of discovering draughtsmen who might be trusted to return to him a block of wood with a fair design pencilled

thereon instead of selling it for a few immediate pence, and of interviewing such artists as called upon him either to solicit employment, to request instant and inordinate reward for work done, or to point out that his engraving of their drawings was "sickening" (I quote the word usually used).

Then he has bought certain machines and engaged accomplished workmen to take off the impressions from the blocks, and, further, to produce such letterpress as may be wanted to accompany the cuts. He has also secured the services of book binders and of those who stitch covers on to regulated masses of printed matter—in short, he has prepared himself to get out and produce in its completeness an illustrated book—plain or in colours.

Now it will be very evident that the employment and direction of so many men and of so much machinery, and the necessary pleadings with publishers, explaining to authors and combats with artists, must unfit a man for quiet steady work such as is required from a true engraver, who should have unclouded eye and unshaking hand.

Therefore E.E., Cooper and others wear tall silk hats, have extensive establishments, and seldom, if ever, touch a block themselves.' (*Yours Pictorially*, p. 104.)

32 [Thomas Bewick]
History of British Birds. The figures engraved on wood by T. Bewick. Vol. I containing the history and description of land birds
Newcastle, printed by Sol. Hodgson, for Beilby & Bewick, 1797. Block size 3¼ × 1½ in. Wood engraving.

'Old age and heedless youth': a brilliant, tiny vignetted "tale-piece", almost Hogarthian in its moral content. The block was engraved after a pencil drawing had been transferred on to its surface. The original drawing, with the folds of the paper still showing, is in the British Museum's Department of Prints and Drawings. It has been worked up by Bewick into a hand-coloured picture.

BL. 672 g 17, p.202

[7] Beatrix Potter commented unfavourably on the 'graininess' which occurred in the printing of Caldecott's penultimate pair of books *Come Lasses and Lads* and *A Farmer Went Trotting*, which she thought may have come from a planographic process. In fact, the same effect occurs as early as *John Gilpin* and was probably a result of Evans's treatment of the surface of the wood-block.

the reproduction of his work and that often, perhaps because of the engraver's incompetence, perhaps because of the artist making too great a demand on the medium, the printed picture did not do justice to the original. It is true also that later printings of a set of illustrations might be spoiled through deterioration of the blocks or through the warping or shrinking of composite blocks (many pictures in the later issues of Caldecott's Toy Books show curious rectangular lines where the joints have given slightly). Nevertheless, the skill and industry of the trade engravers brought into Victorian households a range and quality of illustrations—a consciousness of pictorial expression—that no society had experienced before on such a scale.

Lithography

Where woodcuts and wood engravings are printed from a raised surface, and where metal engravings are printed from an incised surface, lithography allows printing to be done from a flat one—initially, and for many decades, the planed surface of a limestone block. The principle by which it works is the antagonism of oil and water. The artist draws or paints his design with a pen or brush on to the porous stone with a greasy ink. When the stone is flooded with water it will only accept the water on those parts free from ink, and when the stone is rolled with ink it will only accept it on the drawn parts where there is no water. In consequence, paper impressed on the stone will print with the image drawn there.

For a long time after its invention in about 1796 lithography was used for making individual prints, or for plates in books of some prestige (although it is occasionally to be found in the frontispieces or in a few illustrations in children's books). Only in the mid-nineteenth century, when its potential in large-scale colour-printing was realised, did it come to be seen as a medium to rival the wood-block printers. Firms like that of Kronheim combined lithographic work with wood-engraved printing; others, like that of Thomas De La Rue, printed books incidentally to a larger trade in anything from banknotes to playing cards; and, in the last decades of the century, many children's picture books by English designers were printed at the huge lithographic works in Holland (Emrik & Binger) or Germany (Nister) and reimported for sale.

It is curious that the manifest value of the lithographic process—that of allowing the artist to work directly on a printing surface—was not much heeded by the great illustrators of children's books. Certainly the peerless *Book of Nonsense* by Edward Lear was first published by lithography—with some woeful results in its second edition—and occasionally some very attractive books were done in this way. But during the nineteenth century most lithographic productions were run-of-the-mill to the point of vulgarity; the results were neither so exact in delineation nor so subtle in colouring as wood-block printing achieved.[7]

The full significance of lithography as an all-purpose reproductive medium has been discovered by the twentieth century, when the preparation of the surface has come to be allied to photographic methods and when that surface itself has changed from stone to either treated metal or rubber and has been adapted to the mass-production methods of the web-fed rotary press. Some of the masterpieces of modern picture-books figure among the early examples of photolithographic printing: William Nicholson's *Clever Bill* for instance or Edward Ardizzone's *Little Tim and the Brave Sea Captain* (see p. 96), and today almost every example of picture-book art—no matter how the artist has prepared his originals—will be printed by offset lithography.

'Process'

In order to complete this very generalised survey of printing techniques and their effect on the look of picture-books it is necessary to note the emergence in the 1880s of the reproductive method that was to kill the long-standing profession of the engraver. This method—often referred to pejoratively by those engravers as 'process'—entailed the complete production of relief printing surfaces by photo-mechanical methods. The artist's drawing was not only photographed on to the block, but, by using a metal block with a chemically-treated surface, the image could be held in relief while those parts that were not needed could be etched away without any touch from knife.

At its simplest this meant that any black-and-white drawing, properly presented to the camera, could be exactly reproduced—and could even be enlarged or reduced as required. It also led, through the trichromatic process, to the use of the camera in preparing blocks for colour-printing. (One of the very first of these was Beatrix Potter's *Tale of Peter Rabbit*, printed by the firm of Edmund Evans—although the colour-blocks were made by the specialist firm of Hentschel.)

For the artist in black-and-white the arrival of process was a liberating experience, ensuring him a firm control over his drawings and the design of his pages. Its potential was readily perceived by the genius of Aubrey Beardsley (whose fairy tale *Under the Hill*, however, is hardly a children's book) and much of the flowering of new illustrative styles during the period of art nouveau (to say nothing of the jungly undergrowth of decoration for decoration's sake) derives from the eagerness with which black-and-white artists embraced the opportunities which process offered.

The chance to festoon pages with a mixture of picture and decoration is well seen in the ebullient work of Charles Robinson, in such children's books as his edition of Stevenson's *Child's Garden of Verses* (1896) or in his bumper books of fables and fairy stories published by the popular exploiters of art nouveau, Blackie & Sons of Glasgow. At almost the same time the fashion emerged for the making of elaborate 'process' colour-plate books, upon which the reputations of such as Arthur Rackham and Edmund Dulac were founded. The illustrator's art (which might be bundled up into mounted plates, bound in at the end of the book) now comes to be seen as something independent of, and usually more important than, the text that inspired it. Such albums are portents of an inundation of picture books of every shape, size and style, amongst which it has become all too easy to lose not only one's bearings but one's critical discrimination too.

3

William Hogarth and the establishment of English narrative illustration

The tradition of which Randolph Caldecott is such an equable and vigorous representative may be seen as having its beginnings in the fiercely dramatic art of William Hogarth. The connection may at first seem tenuous, or even contrived, but certain characteristics in Hogarth's illustrative work, and in the way that he thought about it, clearly anticipate an attitude that was to be common to generations of illustrators who perforce lived under very different, and sometimes rapidly changing, circumstances.

To begin with, there is the matter of technique. The point has already been made that anyone with ambitions to be an illustrator in the early eighteenth century would hardly confine himself to the cramped and rudimentary expressive range of the woodcut—for all that it had a comfortable appropriateness for many cramped and rudimentary texts. (It is true that it had rendered up unexpected complexities in the hands of such continental masters as Dürer, but by Hogarth's day the making of visual statements meant inescapably the making of prints.) The possibilities of etching for book illustration had already been demonstrated in an English context by Francis Barlow in the plates for Aesop, but it was Hogarth who first exploited the potential of the metal-plate, and who did so with a consciousness of advantages that were much more than commercial.

For Hogarth the making of prints was a direct means of rendering the vitality of the life around him. In his *Analysis of Beauty* of 1753 he early on quotes with approval from a sixteenth-century translation of Lamozzo that 'the greatest grace and life that a picture can have is, that it express Motion' and much of his treatise is a justification of the value which he places on the artist's use of wavy and serpentine lines ('the art of composing well is the art of varying well').

In view of what Maurice Sendak has had to say about the essence of dance in so much of Randolph Caldecott's drawing, it is of more than passing interest to find pre-echoes in these ruminations by Hogarth on technique. When, for instance, in the *Analysis* he speaks of the relationship between the artist's feeling for line and the motion of a worm-jack, he goes on charmingly to recall:

I never forget my frequent strong attraction to it, when I was very young, and that its beguiling movement gave me the same kind of sensation then, which I since felt at seeing a country-dance ...

And, fully bearing out this parallel, when he comes to discuss the techniques of composition he does so with a print of just such a dance (**33**)—containing in it both the compositional grace and the double sense of hilarity (the participants' hilarity and the observer's hilarity) which is to be found in the dance series of *Hey Diddle Diddle* or *The Great Panjandrum Himself*. (Dare one also remark a further compositional parallel? In Hogarth's plate for *Beer Street*, 1751, there is a comic detail of a signpainter up a ladder next to a pastoral pub signboard labelled 'Health to the Barley Mow'. The folk-dancing around the barley-stook and the figure at its peak are pure Caldecott, well and truly back in the eighteenth century.)

It is not simply in his praise for vitality in drawing that Hogarth can be seen as a forerunner of Caldecott, though. There is also the question of the

33 William Hogarth

The Analysis of Beauty. Written with a view of fixing the fluctuating ideas of taste.

London: printed by J. Reeves for the Author, and sold by him at his house in Leicester Fields, 1753. 15 × 19½ in. Engraved folding plate bound in at the end of the text.

The picture was intended by Hogarth to demonstrate certain ideas about technique and composition. Aside from such a utilitarian function it is in itself a salutary example of vigorous narrative picture-making.

BL. 562* b 12. Final plate

pictures themselves. For—as has been widely enough acknowl-edged—Hogarth is the founding-father of English narrative painting,[8] and the several series of moralities that he published in print form are at once the first and the finest examples of storytelling in pictures. Hogarth himself reckoned that the 'ocular demonstration' of the points that he wished to make gained force because 'I have endeavoured to treat my subjects as a dramatic writer, my picture is my stage, etc. . .'.[9] (Introduction to *The Harlot's Progress*, 1733); but no theatrical producer is likely to have filled his set with quite the profusion of moral signposts that Hogarth did. As Sacheverell Sitwell puts it:

> . . . the utmost detail of anecdote has been lavished on every incident depicted. If there is a picture hanging on the wall its subject points the moral, or is a satire upon the play of the figures. No detail is accidental or allowed its entrance without the weight of some meaning upon it. (*Narrative Pictures* (1937), p. 29)

This insistence on the content of pictures, on the telling force of every detail, is a lesson that has been absorbed by the creators of picture books as well as of moral prints, even though it may be thought that there was no place on their territory for the creator of 'Gin Lane' or *Marriage à la Mode*. It so happens however, that Hogarth did produce one series of prints which he said were 'calculated for the instruction of young people' and which (in the best traditions of the bumper book and the *Beano Annual*) 'sell much more rapidly at Christmas than at any other season'.[10]

The series is *Industry and Idleness*, a set of ten plates published in 1747, which, like so much of the children's literature of the period, commended diligence and moral probity by showing how they led to fame and fortune, and condemned loose living by showing how it led to the gallows. Perhaps because the theme did not have the same scope for commenting on social *mores*, as did Hogarth's great didactic series, perhaps because 'the instruction of young people' called for a rather less concentrated set of visual references, *Industry and Idleness* is hardly more subtle than the comparable children's books. Nevertheless, it does bring graphic distinction and an experience of narrative picture-making into a field where such features were noticeably absent (**34**).

Moreover, the influence of the series did not end there. It figured in Dr Trusler's endeavour to 'improve the Minds of Youth' (**35**) by issuing *Hogarth Moralized* in 1768 (of which John Nichols remarked that the author 'was much better qualified to descant on the morality of Mr Penny's pictures, than to set up for the hierophant of Hogarth's genius'). They also found their way into the harlequinade fashion—for the hitherto unknown Book 3 of Robert Sayer's series proves to be a rather feeble adaptation of the story (**36**). And in

[8] See for instance the way he dominates Sacheverell Sitwell's pioneer study of the genre: *Narrative Pictures; a survey of English genre and its painters* (London, 1937).

[9] *cf* Edward Ardizzone: 'I like to think of the illustrator as a kind of stage designer, and, as such, designing the settings for the author's play of character, thereby doing something that the author cannot do in words and also, in a sense, adding another dimension to the book.' ('On the illustrating of books.' *PLA Quarterly*, i:3 (1957), p. 28.)

[10] Quoted from Hogarth's memoranda by John Nichols in *The Works of William Hogarth* (London, 1835–37), p. 23.

the nineteenth century at least two editions of the sequence, with woodcut illustrations, were published, apparently because 'there is not a more proper present to be given by the Chamber of London, at the binding and enrolling an apprentice than a book of this kind' (**37**). By 1824 they had also become subject-matter for use in the *National School Magazine* where a heavy moral commentary is appended to execrable woodcut reductions of Hogarth's originals—with such 'touchy' elements as the prostitute in Plate VII being eliminated.

34 William Hogarth

Industry and Idleness [a series of prints] *design'd & engraved by Wm Hogarth. Publish'd according to Act of Parliament 30 Sept. 1747*

The evolution of Plate I: 'The Fellow Prentices at their Looms'

(a) Hogarth's preliminary drawing. The scene is roughly laid out with ideas for development noted in the margin.
Pen drawing with sepia ink and grey wash.

(b) the finished drawing, ready for transfer to the plate.
Noose and mace have now been incorporated, together with other ideas such as the beer mug.
Mostly drawn with a fine brush in grey and black.

(c) the finished print which has gained a further telling expansion of narrative detail, emphasizing the moral content.
Engraved on copper.
British Museum: Dept of Prints and Drawings. Hogarth Period III vol 6; nos. 24, 25, and Plate I

34(a)

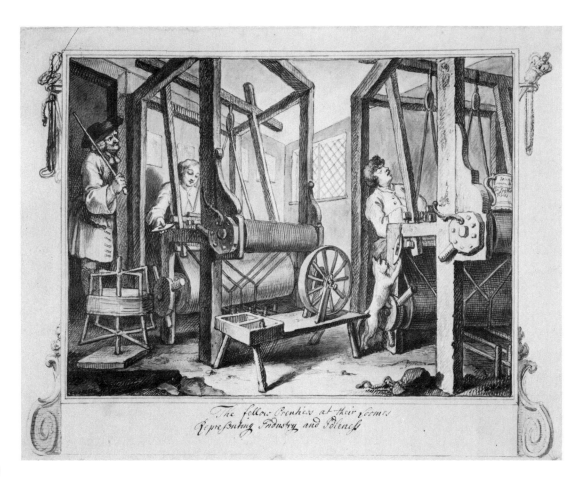

The fellow Prentices at their looms
Representing Industry and Idleness

34(b)

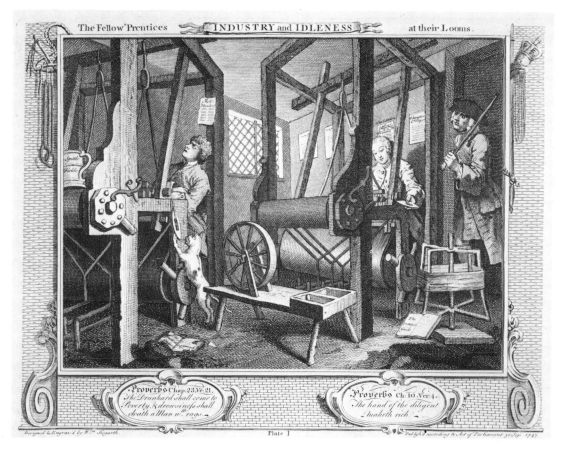

The Fellow'Prentices — INDUSTRY and IDLENESS — at their Looms.

Proverbs Chap:23.Ve:21.
The Drunkard shall come to
Poverty,& drowsiness shall
cloath a Man w.th rags.

Proverbs Ch:10.Ver.4.
The hand of the diligent
maketh rich.

Designed & Engrav'd by W.m Hogarth.   Plate I   Publish'd according to Act of Parliament 30 Sep.r 1747

34(c)

VIEW, then, the noble contraſt; ſee, the fellow 'Prentices, at their looms, in the workſhop of a *Spital-fields* weaver. Obſerve, in the one, a ſerene and open countenance, the diſtinguiſhed mark of innocence; and, in the other, a hanging, down-caſt look, the index of a corrupt and vicious heart. The induſtrious lad is, here, diligently, employed at his work, and, his thoughts, are wholly, taken up with the buſineſs he is upon. His book, called, the *Prentice's Guide*, ſuppoſed to be given him for inſtruction, lies fair and open, beſide him, as peruſed with care, and, attention. The employment of the day ſeems his conſtant ſtudy; and, the intereſt of his maſter, his continual regard. Even, in his leiſure hours, the uſual times of recreation, he is not without a thought on the obligations of his ſtation, but, paſſes his time, in exact conformity to his ſenſe of duty; and, we are given to underſtand, by thoſe ballads, paſted on the wall, behind him, which contain the hiſtories of the *London* 'Prentice, *Whittington*, the Mayor, &c. that if his boyiſh follies, ever lead him to lay out a penny, in youthful amuſements, it is on things that may improve his mind, and, correct his underſtanding. On the contrary, his fellow-'prentice, over-powered with beer, plain, from the half-gallon pot before him, is, with his arms folded, fallen aſleep; a manifeſt

token

35 John Trusler, (ed.)

Hogarth Moralized. Being a complete edition of Hogarth's Works ... calculated to improve the minds of youth

London: sold by S. Hooper ... and Mrs Hogarth, 1768. 9 × 5¼ in. Engraving by Dent, after Hogarth.

The original print is here so shrunk down that Trusler must of necessity explain its content. Gratuitously he adds his own moral reflections.

BL. G2585, p.74

36 [Industry and Idleness]

Publish'd according to Act of Parliament
March 3, 1768 by Robert Sayer ... (Book 3 of
his harlequinade series)

Panel sizes: 7 × 12½ in. Engravings touched with
colour

The scenes in this apparently unique (even
though disbound) copy of a Sayer
harlequinade concentrate upon portraits, with
only a small amount of background detail.
Correspondence with Hogarth's series of
plates is only tenuous.

University of California at Los Angeles Research
Library, Dept of Special Collections

37 [William Hogarth]

*Hogarth's Idle and Industrious Apprentices with
original descriptive poetry*

Derby, Thomas Richardson; London, Simpkin
Marshall, 1834. 7¾ × 4⅞ in. Woodcuts.

The publisher commends this late adaptation
of the original print series with the hopeful
adjuration: 'Give but the boy this history to
peruse, and his future welfare is almost certain'.
The booklet was probably intended to be
distributed to apprentices, and this edition was
preceded by a much scruffier one which
Richardson had published from his earlier
London address in 1829.

University of California at Los Angeles Research
Library, Dept of Special Collections

The fellow-Apprentices at their Looms.

4

William Blake

While the place of Hogarth at the start of a clearly definable illustrative tradition is indisputable, the place of Blake is outside any such simple classification. Against the packed, but ultimately comprehensible, references of Hogarth's moralities, he offers images which still defy interpretation, and he would doubtless have felt nothing but contempt for the gross materialism so explicit in *Industry and Idleness*.

As a man proud of his skill however ('I do not Pretend to Engrave finer than Alb. Durer Goltzius Sadeler or Edelinck but I do pretend to Engrave finer than Strange Woolett Hall or Bartolozzi ... because I understand drawing which they understood not')* he could recognize a fellow-craftsman—as is suggested by his few known comments on Hogarth. Like Hogarth he too was convinced that the drawn line was the foundation of true art:

The great and golden rule of art, as well as of life, is this: that the more distinct, sharp, and wiry the bounding line, the more perfect the work of art; and the less keen and sharp, the greater is the evidence of weak imitation, plagiarism, and bungling ...**

It could have been this commitment to line that was partially responsible for Blake's experimenting with printing processes and his invention of the 'infernal methods' by which he printed his illuminated books.[11] So far as we know, these methods produced an etched plate which left everything that was to be printed as a relief surface and not an intaglio one. The advantage of this to Blake was that it gave him a greater freedom to combine the writing and the illustration of his texts (and a greater sense of participating in the unconventional?) than would be the case if he had simply called upon his skill as a trade engraver.

So it comes about that the first masterpiece of English children's literature, which is also the first great original picture book, stems from an impulse to integrate words and images within a single linear whole. *Songs of Innocence*, printed and published by Blake himself in1789, is the book in which his new technique fully reveals its potential, with every manner of illustrative device being employed, from the purely pictorial frontispiece, to the simple head- or tail-piece illustration, to decorative or symbolic use of small drawings wreathing and interpenetrating the hand-written text.

Like everything else that Blake did, *Songs of Innocence* will not be coralled into any delimited school of illustration. Or rather—such is the intensity of the work—it may be seen as holding the essence of several schools; the plainly pictorial, the decorative, the emblematic, and the narrative. What needs to be emphasised in all this however is that the variety of styles seeks to justify itself by its applicability to the variety of purpose. The symbolic force of the flaming plant in 'The Blossom' (**38**) counterpoints the näivete of the two stanzas of the poem; the pastoral scenes at the head of 'Laughing Song' and the tail of 'Nurse's Song' (**39**) combine force of composition with a grace that aligns them closely with the picture book art that is the subject of this essay.

* The so-called 'Public Address' 1810–11 in Blake's 'notebook' (ed. G.E. Bentley, *William Blake's Writings*, 1978, II, p. 1036).

** from *A Descriptive Catalogue of Pictures* ... London, 1809, pp. 63–4.

[11] For a complete account of Blake's command of graphic processes see Robert N. Essick's *William Blake, Printmaker*. (New Jersey, Princeton University Press, 1980.)

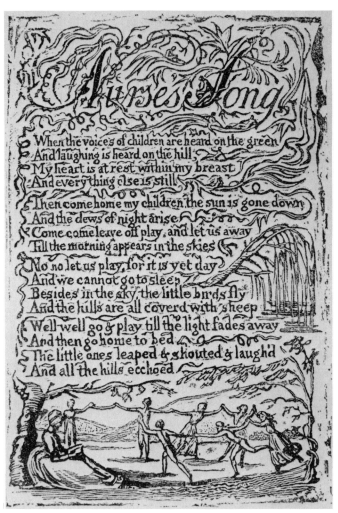

38 William Blake

Songs of Innocence

The Author and Printer W. Blake, 1789. 'The Blossom'. Plate size 4⅛ × 2⅞ in. Copper plate etched in relief and hand-coloured; here reproduced from the Trianon Press facsimile in collotype and stencil, Paris, 1954

The poem etched within the design, and the design itself, carrying an illustrative commentary which suggests that there is more to the words than birds and blossoms.

BL. C102 a.17, plate 28 of this edition.

39 William Blake

[As **38**]

'Nurse's Song': image size 4⅝ × 3⅛ in. Copper plate etched in relief, uncoloured; here reproduced from the electrotype of Blake's original print in Alexander Gilchrist's *Life of William Blake*. London, Macmillan, 1863

A dance scene of wonderful simplicity and vitality, with the titling and the text of the poem packed with symbolic commentary.

BL. 10859 L16 Vol II, plate 9 [i.e. plate 6]

Such festive utterance is hardly to be found in Blake's other book for children (which, so far as we know, only one contemporary child ever saw— for all that Blake did remark to the wretched Dr Trusler that his Visions have particularly 'been Elucidated by Children who have taken a greater delight in contemplating my Pictures than I even hoped').* *For Children The Gates of Paradise*, which announces itself as published in 1793, but which was probably printed and issued as an edition of only a few copies, is an inscrutable work. It is printed from conventionally-engraved plates and its sequence of seventeen powerful images is accompanied by legends of extreme brevity (although these were expanded slightly when the little book was reissued round about 1818, with a 'key', as *For the Sexes the Gates of Paradise*).

*Letter of 23 August 1799 in Bentley (1978) II p.1527.

40 [William Blake]
For Children. The Gates of Paradise
Published by W. Blake … and J. Johnson … 1793.
'Alas!': plate size $3\frac{1}{8} \times 2$ in. Etched and engraved
copper plate here reproduced from the Trianon Press
facsimile in collotype. Clairvaux, 1968

Blake's reworking of a conventional image,
which we have already met above (**31**). In
place of the butterfly Blake puts a fleeting
cherubic spirit whose companion has already
been brought low. When the plate was
reissued in 1818 as *For the Sexes. The Gates of
Paradise* the legend was extended to become:

> What are these? Alas! The Female Martyr
> Is She also the Divine Image

BL. Cup 503 a.31 Vol II, plate 7

For Children is usually referred to as an emblem book, implying that the pictures are open for individual interpretation as a series of moral or meta-physical propositions. This may be so—even though children are unlikely to go to the lengths now demanded by Blake scholarship. On the other hand, the vibrant narrative potential of each picture alongside its verbal signpost and, more especially, the cumulative narrative force of the pictures as a sequence, give the book an integrity that is not found in the often rather random lucubrations of the emblem tradition. Blake—unlike the scholars—credits children with the imaginative gift of Elucidation which may draw unsuspected wonders of storytelling from these pregnant images (**40**).

5

Rowlandson and the arrival of commercial picture books

Blake seems not to have cared very much for Thomas Rowlandson. In the letter to Dr Trusler quoted above he reprimands Nichols's 'hierophant of Hogarth's genius' in words that come a little strangely from the author of *An Island in the Moon*:

I perceive that your Eye is perverted by Caricature Prints, which ought not to abound as much as they do. Fun I love but too much Fun is of all things the most loathsom . . .

And in a letter of explanation to his friend George Cumberland (who had effected the contact between Blake and Trusler) he remarks primly of the Doctor: 'for his own sake I am sorry that a Man should be so enamoured of Rowlandson's caricatures as to call them copies from life & manners or fit Things for a Clergyman to write upon.'

All of which is something of a pity, since, as Dr Robert Wark has pointed out, Blake and Rowlandson were not only exact contemporaries, being born (possibly) and dying (certainly) in the same year as each other, but they shared also a like technical skill in the craft of engraving and they were 'probably the two greatest masters of line drawing that England has produced'. It is of no consequence in that bold assessment that the character of their line drawing is different; that, where Blake sought the distinct, the sharp and the wiry, Rowlandson achieves an irrepressible fluency ('romping, bouncing calligraphy' as Dr Wark so aptly calls it). What matters for the present purpose is that it was the spirit implicit in Rowlandson—though hardly his technique—that stands behind the first major endeavour on the part of publishers to create and exploit a market for what are recognisably 'picture books'. When the English picture book finally arrives on the scene, it does so in close association with the burgeoning of English caricature—and the qualities of that caricature, which had its roots in the skill and vigour of Hogarth, are present in the same measure in most of the great picture books down to the present day.

Three main elements come together here as picture books find a place for themselves at the start of the nineteenth century. In terms of popular taste, there is a public well-accustomed to looking at and interpreting pictures. The growth and widespread popularity of the 'Caricature Prints' that Blake deplored stimulated a demand for pictures of all kinds.

In terms of style there is, in such as Rowlandson (as opposed to the ferocious Gillray), an artistry which combines penetrating observation with a sunny, but also penetrating, wit. And it should not be forgotten that Rowlandson has direct connections with Hogarth, whose *Peregrination* he copied round about 1781, probably for Michael Livesay, who was reproducing Hogarth prints for Mrs Hogarth at her house in Leicester Fields. He is also to be found time and again copying (and learning from?) Hogarth's pictures and illustrations, such as the studies of caricatured heads.

Finally, in terms of production, there is the regularity with which the engraved copper-plate is now coming to be used by graphic artists as a vehicle for expression. The making of plates and, more especially, the colouring of prints by hand, has become an integral part of the changing publishing industry.

The first notable picture book in which these elements came together is

*The quotations from Robert Wark are taken, with permission, from an unpublished lecture on Rowlandson as a draughtsman.

49

The Comic Adventures of Old Mother Hubbard and Her Dog, which was published by J. Harris 'successor to E. Newbery, Corner of St Pauls Church Yard' on 1 June, 1805. It is a square booklet of sixteen leaves, bound in covers of plain coloured paper, titled in letterpress. Both the text and the illustrations of the rhyme are on engraved plates, with the customary result that one side of each leaf is a blank. Copies appear to have been issued without hand-colouring, but early printings are now of such rarity that nothing can be entirely certain.

Except as an historic portent *Old Mother Hubbard* is not a particularly marvellous book. The text, by Sarah Catherine Martin (compiled 'at the suggestion' of John Bastard Esq., M.P. for the County of Devon—perhaps to stop Miss Martin from chattering) is in all probability based on a traditional rhyme. It takes the Dame and her Dog through what has now come to be seen as the usual—but nonetheless tedious and uncoordinated—set of incidents and it pictures these in a manner which, for all its cottage quaintness, is undeniably stilted; much profile drawing to an interior backdrop from a single point of vision, with little attempt to make much of the narrative possibilities. Fortunately though, the unknown engraver was a good man with dogs and the plates are enlivened throughout by the vigorous portrayal of Mother Hubbard's Fido, not least (and this is significant)

> 'When she came back
> He was dancing a Jig.' (**41**)

There had been precedents of a sort for *Old Mother Hubbard*. The tradition

41 S.M.C. [i.e. Sarah Catherine Martin]
The Comic Adventures of Old Mother Hubbard and her Dog

London, John Harris, 1805. 4¾ × 3¾ in. Engraved throughout; reproduced from a photo-litho facsimile of the first edition, published by the Huntington Library, San Marino, California.

The skittish dog here making his first appearance before the world is possibly related to the one that died (see below: no. **83**).

BL. x990/5245 f.12

BABES IN THE WOOD

Regardless of the Orphan's claim,
By love of fatal Ambition led,
Their rightful fortune now his aim,
An Uncle seeks their blood to shed;
Two Ruffians hir'd to do the deed,
Are brib'd with gold to act with speed.

His well meant efforts prove in vain,
The cruel Villian loudly swears,
He'd stab them o'er and o'er again,
Sooner than yield to coward fears,
Walter enrag'd scarce lets him end,
But bids him quick his life defend

And now he hastes to get them food,
Mean while in innocent delight,
They gather Black berries in the Wood,
Till fast approach the shades of night,
With terror and fatigue quite spent,
To artless sorrow they give vent.

As with their friend they travel on,
Now beat their little hearts with joy.
The Girl who thinks the journey long,
Is cheer'd by Walter and the boy.
At length with pleasure they descry
A house of noble aspect nigh.

42 Anon.

Babes in the Wood

[No publisher; no date. c.1804.] Hand-coloured engraving

A harlequinade intended for children. It gives a much-abbreviated version of the traditional ballad and has a happy ending.

University of California at Los Angeles Research Library; Dept of Special Collections. Whole sheet.

[12] It seems likely that Rowlandson would have known the tradition, too, given his own frequent use of *commedia* figures or compromising 'Harlequin' scenes.

of the harlequinade—printed from engraved plates and hand-coloured—had continued into the nineteenth century and even came to include real children's versions among its numbers (**42**).[12] There were also, here and there, some children's books with hand-coloured illustrations and some little engraved books upon which *Mother Hubbard* could have been modelled. There had even been, two years before, a very similar set of verses on *Old Dame Trot and her Comical Cat*, which had not perhaps caught the public taste because it had none of the pictorial elaboration of the copper-plate *Mother Hubbard*. But she it was who touched the nerve, and the pockets, of her contemporaries and very soon after her first appearace a band-waggon was on the move. John Harris claimed to have sold 10,000 copies of the booklet in a few months after publication, and, as is the way with publishers, both he and his rivals capitalised on the success. Small square engraved booklets 'charmingly embellished' rolled out of the presses and from under the hands of the professional colourists ('one shilling plain, and eighteen-pence coloured'). The hitherto somewhat dowdy world of children's books was never to be the same again.

With the rapid proliferation of books modelled on the production formula of *Old Mother Hubbard* it is to be entirely expected that there should be variation and development in both the subjects chosen and their illustrative treatment. It is to be expected too, that there should be changes in the formula itself, and by 1819 a larger format picture book—measuring 7"x4" instead of the customary 5"x4"—came into fashion, using letterpress text, with illustrations that might be either metal- or wood-engravings. Within the multitude of possibilities that these developments opened up therfore one

D *danc'd for it.* d

THE APPLE PIE.

C   D

c Cried for it.

d Danced for it.

43(a)

43(

43

(a) 'Z'

The History of the Apple Pie; written by Z

London ... for I. Harris, June 25, 1808. 4 × 3¼ in.
Engraved throughout.
Private collection, f.[5]

(b) 'Z'

The History of an Apple Pie ...

London ... for Harris and Son, 1820. 7 × 3¾ in.
Engraved, hand-coloured illustration, letterpress text
BL. c 95 b 6, f.[3]

The engraving for the 1820 edition may be
harsher than its predecessor, with fairly coarse
colouring, but it has more ingenuity and
liveliness. (The young miss in the first example
may well be sister to the one in *The Elegant
Girl: 13* above.)

may trace for the first time the emergence of varied stylistic characteristics
jostling for attention in the market place—and on the critic's table.

The flat stageiness found in *Old Mother Hubbard* recurs for instance in
Harris's first edition of *The History of an Apple Pie*, published in 1808 (**43**(a))—
and, indeed, he may have been conscious of its rather static simplicity, for he
had some much more vigorous woodcuts made for it when he reissued it in
the larger format in 1820 (**43**(b)). Elsewhere there are to be found improve-
ments on this elementary pictorialization either through attempts at more
fluent engraving (**44**), or through bolder attempts at comedy (**45**) or through
a modest interpretive charm (**46**).

Although many were reproduced from copper plates, few of these little
books related very closely to the tradition of caricature within which
Rowlandson was working. They incorporate here and there humorous
touches and gestures which are part of the fun of children's picture books, but
one needs to look at some of the commentaries on character (**47**) or some of
the more satirical ventures (which may not have been intended for children at
all) to see the presence of an influence from Rowlandson. Indeed, the great

man's name itself is upon at least one of the picture books of the period (**48**)—although the crassness of the text makes one hope that he had nothing more to do with it than etching the plates—and at least one other book has been attributed to him (**49**). The publisher of this, Thomas Tegg, issued many prints in the production of which Rowlandson was involved towards the end of his life, and it is therefore surprising to find him not advertising his artist when he had the chance. It may well be that *Peter Pry's Puppet Show*, with other books from the same stable, like *The Loves of Mr Jenkins and Polly Pattens* (1809) were merely done 'in the Rowlandson manner' by someone in Tegg's shop.

44 Anon.
A True History of a Little Old Woman who Found a Silver Penny
London, printed for Richard Phillips, 1812. Spread: 5 × 8 in. Hand-coloured engraving.

The story illustrated is the well-known one of the pig who would not jump over the stile, and after each separate incident had been pictured the whole cumulation was repeated in a single panorama at the end of the book (defective in the British Library copy). The plates for this 1812 edition were first used in Benjamin Tabart's 1806 printing and are little more than rough sketches apparently done in haste. Editions with re-engraved, or more fully detailed, pictures also exist.
BL. ch 800/111 (6), ff.[6-7]

"O wait my dear Giant; first drink some strong wine,
Then on that dainty you may afterwards dine.
He seiz'd a large cup and tippled so deep,
That he tumbled down flat and fell fast asleep.

Soon as Jack saw him fall, he crept from the bed,
Then snatch'd a large knife and chopt off his head:
Thus he kill'd this great Man, as he loudly did snore,
And never again was a Giant seen more.

45 B.A.T.

The History of Mother Twaddle . . .

London, John Harris, 1807. 5 × 8½ in. Engraved and hand-coloured throughout.

A versified account of 'Jack and the Beanstalk', published in the same year as the first, but much less sprightly, prose version.

BL. ch 800/111 (1) ff.[13–14]

46 Trad.

The History of the House that Jack Built . . .

London, Harris & Son, 1820. 7 × 4¾ in. Hand-coloured wood engraving.

An example of one of Harris's larger format 'Cabinet' books. The rhyme has been extended beyond the normal version, which was that chosen by Caldecott for his 1878 edition.

BL. 012806 ee 31 (3). Final page.

This is Sir John Barley-corn, that treated the Boy that every morn, swept the Stable snug and warm, that was made for the Horse of a beautiful form, that carried Jack with his Hound and Horn, that caught the Fox that lived under the Thorn, that stole the Cock that crowed in the morn, that waked the Priest all shaven and shorn, that married the Man all tattered and torn, that kissed the Maiden all forlorn, that milked the Cow with the crumpled Horn, that tossed the Dog, that worried the Cat, that killed the Rat, that eat the Malt, that lay in the House that Jack built.

46

Yawning is catching.

Upon a large Forest and under a Hill,
Was placed by a Stream a small water Mill,
At the head of the Brook there was a large Bog,
And the Man of the Mill was call'd Billy Hog,
His Figure was odd his Senses not great,
And he carried a wig on his very bald Pate,
With a crooked back and a timber leg,
When the Mill did not go was oblig'd to beg.

47 Anon.

Peter Prim's Pride; or proverbs that will suit the young or the old

London, J. Harris, 1810. 5¼ × 4¼ in. Hand-coloured engraving with stippling.

The caricaturing, the style of engraving and the blend of colours suggest an influence from Rowlandson. The stylishness of the presentation, with all the emphasis on the foregrounded figures, contrasts with the simpler line-work seen in the previous examples from this period.

BL. ch 810/47, facing p.4

48. Anon.

The History of Billy Hog and his Wife Margery. A true story, as the readers may choose to believe, purposely invented for the amusement of children, by an Old Fellow. The plates etched by Rowlandson.

London, P. Martin, 1816. Approx. 4¼ × 3½ in. Collection of Mr and Mrs J. Lapides, Baltimore.

49 Anon.

Peter Pry's Puppet Show for Good Children

London, T. Tegg, n.d. (1810). Etched throughout with hand-colouring

The etchings were attributed to Rowlandson (without citations) when the book was sold at Sotheby's on 2 June 1982 (catalogue no. 215).

By kind permission of Sotheby's.

Here's Mr. Punch and Joan his Wife,
True friends of fun and glee Sir,
A Song, or dance, or merry glee,
Just suit them to a T. Sir.

6

The Cruikshanks and transition

The arrival of Thomas Tegg here serves the further purpose of linking to Rowlandson the name of another draughtsman, who surely ranks very close to him in his command of drawing: George Cruikshank. Precocious (he claimed to have contributed to etchings done by his father when he was six or seven years old, prolific (the bibliography of his very varied work runs to well over 2,000 entries), Cruikshank experienced early on in his long and choppy career associations with both Gillray and Rowlandson. He not only met the former, but also completed plates for him when he had become incapacitated; and—through Tegg—he engaged in etching caricatures by George Woodward, that figured alongside Rowlandson's. He was also asked to provide illustrations to harmonise with some of Rowlandson's in Tegg's *Wit's Magazine* of 1818. (To complete so abbreviated a summary of Cruikshank's pedigree in the tradition of caricature [13]one might note also that he was asked to etch four small drawings after Hogarth for the edition of the *Works* that John Major published in 1831.)

Although, at thirteen years of age, even George Cruikshank was a trifle young to be much involved with the first picture books that followed the 1805 *Old Mother Hubbard*, he does claim a fleeting relationship with the movement through his close association with his brother Robert a little later on. It is known that George and Robert between them provided the folding frontispieces for Dean & Munday's series of popular tales (**50**) and it is likely that George had a hand in (or influence on) the engravings that Robert made for the satirical picture books put out by John Marshall on the subject of 'the

[13]'I was cradled in caricature', he is quoted as saying by 'Cuthbert Bede' in his personal recollections of the artist.

Jack and the Bean Stalk

Jack cutting down the Bean and the Ogre's Fall.

Jack running away with the Ogre's Money Bags.

Jack's Narrow Escape with the Ogre's Harp.

51 Anon.

*The Dandies' Ball; or high life in the city.
Embellished with sixteen coloured engravings*

London, John Marshall, 1819. 7 × 8½ in. Hand-
coloured wood engravings.

The heavily exaggerated cartoon style of
drawing is matched by bright colouring, which
was a characteristic of Marshall's picture books
at this time. The verse form verges on that of
the limerick, which was to make its first known
appearance within a year of this book, when
John Harris published his *History of Sixteen
Wonderful Old Women*, a title quickly imitated
by Marshall.

BL. c 95 b 1, pp.[7–8]

At dinner so pleas'd,

For his mind was quite eas'd,

As all his new clothes were just come,

Sat our dear Mr. Parrot,

Till, carving a carrot,

He unhappily put out his thumb.

While sipping his tea,

Mr. Frill, you may see,

And his friend, both so gaily drest out,

For Mr. Pillblister's

And his polite sister's

Most splendid and elegant rout.

50 Anon.

*The Surprising History of Jack and the Beanstalk.
Embellished with a coloured frontispiece*

London, Dean & Munday, n.d. [1820]. 5⅛ × 8¼ in.
Hand-coloured etched and engraved frontispiece.

George and Robert Cruikshank provided a
number of the composite narrative
frontispieces that Dean & Munday used in this
'fairy tale library', which began publication in
1819.

BL. ch 820/28 (2). Frontispiece.

Dandies' (**51**). Certainly George was in the business of making fun of absurd
fashions and the series of 'Monstrosity Prints' that he made between 1816
and 1826 includes some delectable studies of unfortunate children togged
out in ridiculous costumes.

So far as children's picture books are concerned, however, George is only a
marginal figure (his revolutionary etchings for the first English edition of the
Grimms' *German Popular Stories* and his clever composite plates for such
books as Basile's *Pentamerone* and his own 'Fairy Library' hardly counting as
picture books). Something of the zest that he could have imparted to the
genre can be seen in his *Comic Alphabet* (**52**) and in another panorama, the
Comic Multiplication where his drawings have been lithographed in a rather
gritty fashion. The booklet is undated and may have been done in response
to what George saw as a dishonest use of the family name by his nephew
Percy. This occurred in a series of crudely comic picture books which Percy
did for the firm of Read & Co, who advertised them as by 'Cruikshank'.
Among them was the lithographed panorama of *John Gilpin*, which must
count as one of the most cheerfully energetic treatments to precede
Randolph Caldecott's classic interpretation of 1878 (**53**).

In the main however, once the creative energy inspired by *Mother Hubbard* had spent itself, the children's book trade relapsed (as is always its wont)
into undistinguished and debased imitation. For twenty years or so firms like
those of D. Carvalho, who seems to have built up his business by taking over
the copyrights of the picture books originated through John Marshall, and
the mass-market publishers J. L. Marks (**54**), and, ubiquitously, Thomas Dean
& Son churned out a host of versions of folk tales, nursery rhymes and 'classic
titles' such as Isaac Watts's 'Divine and Moral Songs' and William Roscoe's
The Butterfly's Ball. (The last had originally featured as one of the best-sellers

52 George Cruikshank

A Comic Alphabet, designed, etched and published by George Cruikshank

No 23 Myddleton Terrace, Pentonville, 1836. 5⅛ × 6¾ in. Hand-coloured etching throughout; reproduced from a facsimile published by the Arts Council of Great Britain, 1981.

A later manifestation of Cruikshank's enjoyment of 'the Rowlandson manner'. It does not seem to have been anywhere noticed, but around this time his brother Robert also published a *Comic Alphabet* on similar lines through the firm of Darton & Clark.

53 William Cowper

Cowper's Diverting History of John Gilpin, with twenty illustrations by Percy Cruikshank

London, Read & Co., n.d. [c.1855]. 5½ × 6 in. Lithographic drawing and tinting, with hand-colouring added.

A work not to be underestimated in the history of picture-book art (even though it may have been modelled on the little-known *Comic Multiplication* that Percy's Uncle George published through Ackermann's School of Artistic Industry for [fairly incompetent] Ladies). The application of caricature to a panoramic book — a sense of movement achieved through changing scenes — coupled with the free graphic style results in a cheerful informality that is very suitable for the subject.

BL. 1586/4921, panels [7–9]

X
Xantippe

Y
Yawning

His horse, who never in that sort
  Had handled been before,
What thing upon his back had got
  Did wonder more and more.

Then might all people well discern
  The bottles he had slung;
A bottle swinging at each side,
  As hath been said or sung.

r nought,

set out.

The wind did blow, the cloak did fly,
  Like streamer long and gay,
Till loop and button failing both,
  At last it flew away.

The dogs did bark, the children scream'd
  Up flew the windows all;
And ev'ry soul cried out "Well done!"
  As loud as he could bawl.

Away went Gilpin—who but he?
  His fame soon spread around—
He carries weight! he rides a race!
  'Tis for a thousand pound.

Jack and Jill went up the hill,
To fetch a pail of water,
Jack fell down and broke his crown
And Jill came tumbling after.

Little Jack Horner, sat in a corner,
Eating of Christmas pie,
He, with his thumb. took out a plum,
And said what a good boy am I.

Buy baby bunting,
Daddy's gone a hunting,
To get a little Hare skin,
To wrap a baby bunting in.

Pat-a-cake, pat-a-cake, Baker's man;
So I will master as fast as I can,
Pat it, and prick it, and mark it with T,
Put it in the oven for Tommy and me.

54 Anon.

The Nursery Rhymes, Illustrated

London, printed and puplished [*sic*] by S. Marks & Sons n.d. [1876?] (Grandpa's New Coloured Series). 6¾ × 9 in. Woodcuts.

Despite the series title this is not a 'new' book, being a late reprint of a work long current in the Marks' family list. Nor is it notably 'coloured', although some stencilled tints have been put on the title-page. If the British Library's dating is correct then this survival from a past age would probably have been available alongside the first of the Caldecott Toy Books.

BL. 12314 i 33 (11), pp.[6–7]

in John Harris's engraved series where, in 1807, it was paukily illustrated with charming humanised animals by the young Mulready, and then, in 1808, re-illustrated in drearier, natural-historical, style by an unnamed engraver.)

The most startling legacy from these early picture books in fact derives less from any illustrative feature than from a verse-form: the limerick, as embodied in the *Anecdotes and Adventures of Fifteen Gentlemen*, published about 1821 by John Marshall and, once again illustrated by Robert Cruikshank. This, along with *A Peep at the Geography of Europe. Illustrated by Comic Figures*, probably by the same team, were done in imitation of the first-ever collection of what we now call limericks: *The History of Sixteen Wonderful Old Women*, published with stipple engravings by John Harris in 1820. It was the *Old Gentlemen* however who were known to Edward Lear and who inspired him to make up similar verses for the children of the Earl of Derby—which verses eventually appeared with his own lithographed drawings in the *Book of Nonsense* of 1846 (**55**).

There was an Old Man of the West,
Who wore a pale plum-coloured vest;
When they said, " Does it fit?"
He replied, " Not a bit!"
That uneasy Old Man of the West.

There was an Old Man of the West,
Who never could get any rest;
So they set him to spin
On his nose and his chin,
Which cured that Old Man of the West.

55 Derry-Down-Derry [i.e. Edward Lear]
Book of Nonsense

No publisher, no date, [i.e. T. McLean, 1855].
6 × 9 in. Lithographed throughout.

Three typical limericks and drawings from the
second edition of the *Book of Nonsense*. These
examples have been chosen partly to show
Lear's incomparable zest as a maker of words
and pictures, and partly for technical reasons.
The technique for transferring a typographic
text on to a lithographic stone seems to have
been imperfectly mastered so that in (a) and (b)
we find the two Men of the West being given
each other's limericks; while in (c) the final line
has had to be filled in with a bodged attempt
at imitating italic type.

Private collection. No pagination.

There was a Young Lady of Clare,
Who was sadly pursued by a bear;
When she found she was tired,
She abruptly expired,
That Unfortunate Lady of Clare

Like Blake—but at the other end of the spectrum—Lear is unclassifiable. The *jeu d'esprit* which is the nonsense book comes from the pen of a man who was a master of bird and animal portraiture, and who was to make his living as a landscape painter, and yet it owes nothing whatever to his formal work or to any school of comic art. The hasty sketches, which hardly lost any of their spontaneity in the woodcut versions that succeeded the lithographed editions, have a richness of life and character which is belied by their apparently casual lines. They represent a highly individual adaptation of modes of caricature, perfectly complementing the caricature implicit in the verses, and although they inspired some pleasantly off-beat imitations (**56**) they stand aside from, and above, any other work of their time.

56 [Charles H. Ross]
Rummical Rhymes with Pictures to Match Set Forth in Fayre Prospect Alphabetically and Geographically

London, Dean & Son, n.d. [1864]. 8¼ × 11 in. Woodcuts and letterpress printed in black and red.

One of several facetious picture books written by Charles Ross and illustrated by J.V. Barrett which were inspired by Lear's example. The addition of a second colour to text and pictures may have attracted custom but it does little to enhance the comic effects.

BL. 12808 bbb 4, f.20

HOME DUTIES.

A SINGULAR person of Uske,
   Who always walked out in the Dusk,
Said, at Home she must keep
Till her Bird went to sleep,
Which never occurr'd until Dusk.

UNAPPRECIATED.

A WEARISOME Man of Versailles,
   Was addicted to telling long Tales;
But ne'er found a Friend
Who would list to the end
Of the Stories he told at Versailles.

7

'Alfred Crowquill' and the *Punch* men

The way forward for children's picture books in the Victorian period was to be found through the interdependence of increasingly specialised publishing houses and increasingly active firms devoted to wood-engraving 'for the trade'. It is possible to argue that Alfred Forrester, who published most of his work (sometimes with his brother, Henry) as 'Alfred Crowquill', stands as a transitional figure in this development.

Before delineating his position more clearly however, it is necessary to note one influence from Abroad that was to be of significance in the development of the English tradition. This was the arrival in 1848 of the first English translation of Heinrich Hoffman's classic satire on the moral tale: *Struwwelpeter*, or, as the title character came to be called, 'Shock-headed Peter'.

Struwwelpeter had originally appeared in Frankfurt in 1845, the work of an amateur (Hoffmann was a doctor who made the book as a present for his son). The text and the outline drawings were printed by lithography, the pictures then being hand-coloured, and it was in this way that the English edition was prepared. The books were imported into Britain for sale by an agent (**57**).

Hoffmann's curiously ambivalent treatment of the follies of youth was immensely successful and prompted a rash of imitations, none of which measured up to the original and some of which typically exaggerated its attitude to a point where the ludicrous became horrific (**58**). In a more positive way, however, the book has double importance. First, as Maurice Sendak has pointed out, with what seems like immoderate enthusiasm: 'Graphically it is one of the most beautiful books in the world'—a judgement inspired perhaps by its dynamic design, both as a whole and in its individual leaves, with their varied modes of embodying narrative. The book includes conventional step-by-step portrayals, strip cartoons, and composite pictures which show the stages of the action in a single unified design. Second, the book breaks new ground in its size, for it is the first best-seller to be produced in what might be called quarto format instead of the—at the time—more conventional tall or square octavo. *Struwwelpeter* was to give a new generation of picture-book artists, such as Alfred Crowquill, a more generous page-size within which to organise a balanced relationship between text and picture. Indeed, Crowquill's picture books were advertised as 'uniform in size with *The Struwwelpeter*'.

Crowquill, who came from a City family of some means, appears to have begun his pleasantly amateurish career under the wing of George Cruikshank. Prints and books from the 1820s—mostly harmless comic stuff for adults rather like forerunners of *1066 and All That*—are to be found devised by Crowquill but with the illustrations etched by Cruikshank (later there were to be woodcuts made by the outcast Percy). Crowquill's manner also suggests a Cruikshankian influence—diluted in both the decisiveness of line and the outrageousness of the comedy, but with the same enjoyment of the ridiculous.

It is only much later, however, in the post-Struwwelpeter era, that Crowquill turned his attention to writing and illustrating children's books. This was after he had toyed with illustrations for magazines like *Punch* and the *Illustrated London News* and had perhaps come into contact with the specialist engraving firms who supplied the blocks from which the illustrations were printed. (*Punch* had, in fact, been founded by a master-engraver, Ebenezer

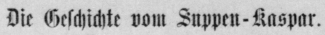

Die Geschichte vom Suppen-Kaspar.

Der Kaspar, der war kerngesund,
Ein dicker Bub und kugelrund,
Er hatte Backen roth und frisch;
Die Suppe aß er hübsch bei Tisch.
Doch einmal fing er an zu schrei'n:
„Ich esse keine Suppe! Nein!
Ich esse meine Suppe nicht!
Nein, meine Suppe eß' ich nicht!"

Am nächsten Tag, — ja sieh nur her!
Da war er schon viel magerer.
Da fing er wieder an zu schrei'n:
„Ich esse keine Suppe! Nein!
Ich esse meine Suppe nicht!
Nein, meine Suppe eß' ich nicht!"

Am dritten Tag, o weh und ach!
Wie ist der Kaspar dünn und schwach!
Doch als die Suppe kam herein,
Gleich fing er wieder an zu schrei'n:
„Ich esse keine Suppe! Nein!
Ich esse meine Suppe nicht!
Nein, meine Suppe eß' ich nicht!"

Am vierten Tage endlich gar
Der Kaspar wie ein Fädchen war.
Er wog vielleicht ein halbes Loth, —
Und war am fünften Tage todt.

57 Heinrich Hoffman

Der Struwwelpeter; oder lustige Geschichten und drollige Bilder

Frankfurt a.M., Literarische Anstalt n.d. 12½ × 10 in. Hand-coloured lithographs.

The celebratory 100th edition of this classic commentary on juvenile behaviour, showing, in this instance, how Hoffmann uses an image sequence to depict passing time and to add symbolic meaning (note how the table shrinks as well as Kaspar). Those who accuse Hoffmann of being a serious moralist may like to compare Kaspar's rapid demise with that of Belloc's string-masticator, Henry King.

BL. 12839 b 13, f.17

58 Anon.

Funny Physic to Cure Bad Habits

London, Dean & Son, n.d. [1858] (No 5 of Dean's Sixpenny Coloured Picture English Struwwelpeters). 9½ × 7¼ in. Hand-coloured wood engraving.

Openly horrific and tacitly anti-Semitic this Awful Warning against biting shows the English perfectly willing to outdo Hoffmann in cautionary rhymes. The publishers were clearly fond of the picture for they later used it in a picture book about slatterns and gluttons: *The Laughable Looking Glass for Little Folks* by Hain Friswell, illustrated by W. McConnell.

There were at least twelve titles in the series to which *Funny Physic* belongs — 6-leaf cheapjack imitations of the Hoffmann formula, with the four pages of their endpapers covered with advertisements for Educational and Religious Publications.

BL. 12807 g 74 (5), f.[1]

THE OLD MAN THAT DRAWS THE TEETH OF CHILDREN WHO BITE.

Tread! tread! tramp! tramp!
Closer and closer I hear his stamp:
In his box are packed,—dreadful freight,—
Full fifty pounds weight,

NAUGHTY CHILDRENS TEETH

1 MILE to HOME

Of the teeth of the children who, sad to relate,
(You'll scarcely believe it,) were given to biting
Each other,—like wild beast in carnage delighting.

Landells, in association with a printer in what was—for them—the forlorn hope that a magazine of their own would ensure steady work for their businesses.)

The strengths and weaknesses of Crowquill's work (and the German influence) can be seen at once in the picture books that he produced for the firm that had taken over John Harris's publications: Grant & Griffith (later Griffith & Farran). These had such titles as *Funny Leaves for the Younger Branches, by Baron Krakemsides of Burstenoudelafen* (n.d., 1852) and *Gruffel Swillendrinken Or the Reproof of the Beasts* (n.d., 1856) and they achieve a very precarious balance between moral earnestness and levity. The first—though you would not guess it from the title—is a verse tale in which a big-game hunter dreams that the elephants get their own back on him: the second is a tract on total abstinence that must have pleased the heart of Crowquill's old master, Cruikshank. In both instances however, the moral lesson of the book is

THE OBSTINATE FROG [CONTINUED.]

That night the young toad hopped away in the dark—
 He thought it a very good joke,
Thus to leave his fond parents, who loved him so well,
 Without giving one farewell croak.
He hopped over hill, and he hopped over dale;
 He struggled through many a bog;
He laughed to himself as he thought how they'd stare
 When they missed him—the wicked young frog.
At last the moon broke, and he saw the great lake,
 That seem'd to run up to the sky,
He thought himself there, but he wasn't just right,
 For it was not so very nigh.

'Twas gained, and he stood on the slippery sand,
 And he looked on the moving wave,
That seemed to talk low, as it heaved and rolled—
 And he did not feel quite so brave.
He thought how they'd laugh if he did return home,
 So he took a refreshing dive,
He soon was thrown back, with a scornful fling;
 But he did not come out alive.
His parents they grieved, and they sought out his corpse,
 Which they bore from the fatal sands;
And dug a small grave, deep amidst the tall reeds,
 Where still his small monument stands.

MORAL.
How many may think that a parent's advice
 Is a stupid and old fashioned clog;
But let them take care, or they soon may be like
 The sad disobedient frog.

5.

59 'Alfred Crowquill' [i.e. Alfred Henry Forrester]
Picture Fables
London, Grant & Griffith, n.d. [1854]. 10 × 8 in.
Hand-coloured wood engraving.

Frogs have an honoured place in the history of the English picture book. These, from an invented verse-fable, have a character and a comedy of expression that fits them happily into a tradition that will later include Charles Bennett, Randolph Caldecott, Beatrix Potter and the American, Arnold Lobel.
BL. 12305 g 2, f.5

moderated by touches of humour in the text, by the liveliness with which Crowquill draws and composes his pictures, and by the brightness and charm of the hand-colouring (**59**).

Around this time Crowquill also appears to have fallen in with the young and busy engraving firm run by the Dalziel Brothers, who had been trying to persuade Richard Doyle to produce a series of fairy-tale picture books. Crowquill possibly filled the gap. He designed (and wrote, in rather stolid fashion) the traditional tales in 'Aunt Mavor's Nursery Tales for Good Little People' which were printed by the Dalziels for the firm that was to dominate picture-book publishing for much of the rest of the century: George Routledge & Co. (**60**).

The pattern which one sees here of an artist/illustrator developing contacts with engraving houses and with the publishers of magazines and books is one which came to dominate much of the trade from this time on. It can be

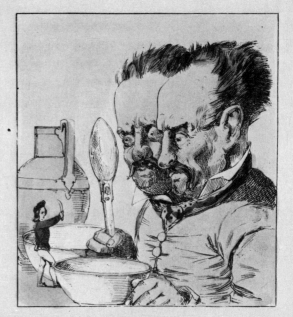

Jack went thro' a wood on his road to Wales, and slept by a well side: some-thing scratch'd his legs and face, and he a-woke a-gain. He was be-ing drag-ged thro' the bri-er-y wood by that ve-ry Giant Blun-der-bore, who drank all his wa-ter from the well where Jack was a-sleep. He threw the boy into a blood-y room full of bones and sculls, and said, "Be ea-sy there, till I sharp-en a knife; what so nice as a lit-tle boy's heart! and who but my own sweet self knows how to cook the same!" He went for a-no-ther Gi-ant to come to dine with him. Some-where all round, Jack heard peo-ple groan-ing: he went to the win-dow and the two Gi-ants were co-ming a-long at a full trot;—they were arm in arm:—now Jack by luck found two ropes in the room, so he made loops, and when the Gi-ants reached the door, he threw a loop o-ver each head;—he put the o-ther end to a beam and pul-led might-i-ly. The Gi-ants' fa-ces went all co-lours, and then turn-ed as black as a ditch. Jack sli-ded down the rope, kill-ed them with his sword, took their keys, and loos-ed all the pri-son-ers. Two poor la-dies were

Jack was tir-ed and he knock-ed at the door of a large stone house, and who should o-pen the door but a tall Gi-ant, with two heads: He gave Jack some sup-per and put him in the best bed, but he heard the Gi-ant say-ing

"Tho' you sleep with me this night,
You shall not see the morning's light."

And sure e-nough when it was dark, in crept the art-ful Gi-ant with a club and beat a-way, but Jack was safe un-der the bed; what the Gi-ant hit was a large sheep-skin bag fill-ed with bran, which Jack found in the room. In the morn-ing Jack went to the Gi-ant's ta-ble and ask-ed for his break-fast. "Hall-o-a!" said the Gi-ant; "Pray how did you sleep last night?" "Pret-ty well," said Jack, "on-ly the rats switch-ed me with their long tails." The Gi-ant fill-ed two bowls with Stir-a-bout:—Jack la-dled all his in-to a lea-ther bag down in his bo-som:—when the Gi-ant had done and wip-ed his mouth, "Look here, Taf-fy!" said Jack, "see what I can do!" and he cut the bag and let the Stir-a-bout on the floor. "Od splut-ter hur nails!" said the Gi-ant; "Hur can do that!" and with his knife he rip-ped his stom-ach up; and of course

60 'Alfred Crowquill' [i.e. Alfred Henry Forrester]

Aunt Mavor's Nursery Tales for Good Little People, comprising [12 titles] *with one hundred illustrations*

London, George Routledge & Co., 1856. 10½ × 15 in. Hand-coloured wood engraving.

A bound-up collection of tales, also issued as separate 16-page picture books. The stolid text, which is made almost unreadable by being divided up into syllables, is offset by the consistent energy of Crowquill's illustrations.

BL. 12806 g 54, pp.[3–4]

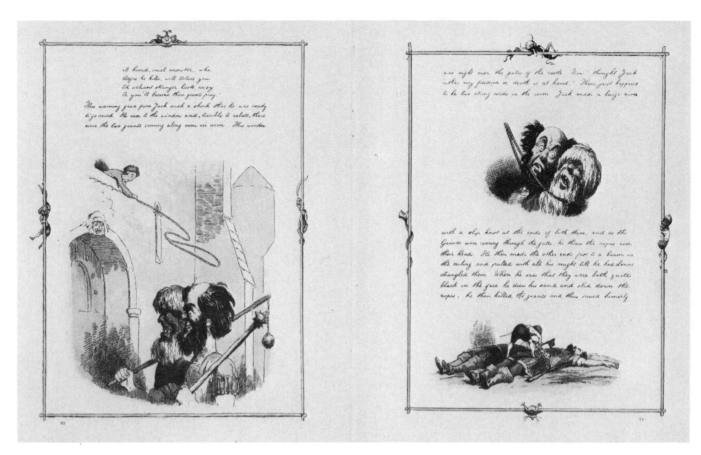

61 Richard Doyle

The Marvellous History of Jack the Giant Killer,
1842 [reproduced in facsimile]

London, Eyre & Spottiswoode, 1888. 9¼ × 7⅞ in.
Lithographic reproduction of a hand-coloured ms.

Like his *Journal* (**6** above) this picture story-
book was one of Doyle's inspired juvenile
works. He was eighteen years old when he
wrote and illustrated it for the entertainment
of the rest of his family. Note how his
eagerness for comedy leads him to invent
acrobatic creatures exercising themselves on
the rustic framework round the text.

BL. 12806 u 32, pp.10–11

seen in one aspect in the wake of the man whom Crowquill possibly super-
seded and who had all Crowquill's zest for drawing, but without his compulsion to burden his pages with trite and obvious moral sentiments: the artist
Richard Doyle.

Like George Cruikshank, Doyle was brought up in a household where art
was—almost—the measure of all things. His father was the mild-mannered
caricaturist who, as ⊞, achieved fame for his polite jokes about the figures
of the day, and we have already seen (p. 15 above) not only how the young
Richard showed an early pleasure in making illustrations, but also how he
used his own enthusiasm for looking at prints as a subject for his drawing. His
national fame as an illustrator arose from his position as a caricaturist for
Punch, whose staff he joined in 1843 at the age of nineteen and for which he
designed the celebrated cover that was to last for over one hundred years.

There can be little doubt that Doyle had it in him to become the great
picture-book illustrator of the nineteenth century. His feeling for line was
instinctive and his fund of comic ideas abundant, as can be seen from yet
another 'family book' that he made in his youth and that was printed in
facsimile after his death (**61**). But a combination of circumstances prevented
that wished-for event from occurring. They are circumstances that arose in
part from the period when Doyle was most active, which was still, in publishing terms, 'transitional'. A clear market for the kind of book that Doyle might
have illustrated was still to be established. At the same time though, Doyle's
rupture with *Punch* over his colleague Douglas Jerrold's violent anti-
Catholicism, coupled with what may well have been an inherited temperamen-
tal flaw, caused him to neglect or lose confidence in his own potential. As

Complaining about Doyle's
unreliability in their (also unreliable)
memoirs, the Dalziel Brothers tell how he
only finished his panoramic *Overland
Journey to the Great Exhibition* (1851) after
the Exhibition had closed. Given the
virtuoso performance of draughtmanship
embodied in that work they had good
reason to be cross.

a result we find a scatter of virtuoso drawings, such as those which he made
for 'The Sleeping Beauty' (**62**), or those for fairy subjects (to be discussed
later: p. 105) but these exist in a text-less limbo and find support only from
factitious, *post hoc* additions.[14]

One curiosity, published posthumously, indicates something of what
Doyle might have done. It is a manuscript 'drawn to amuse some little
children' towards the end of his life. Despite the shakiness of the line, it shows
that Richard Doyle would have been quite able to find within himself a leaner
form of composition than was usual in his richly composed but crowded
style. And—entirely coincidentally—it forces a comparison with one of
Doyle's latterday admirers (**63, 64**).

62 J.R. Planché
*An Old Fairy Tale Told Anew in Pictures and
Verse*, [illustrated by] *Richard Doyle, the pictures
engraved by the Brothers Dalziel*

London, George Routledge & Sons, n.d. [1865].
9 × 7 in. Wood engraving.

Doyle's difficulty in preparing a completely
successful book is exemplified here (and see
also **99** below). The illustrations show his
mastery at organising a drawing packed full of
incident and comic detail, but the text for it
had to be supplied at a later date. Planché in
fact not only put the story into verse but also
added italicized (and redundant) descriptions of
the illustrations.

BL. 11650 f 10, p.17

He says it again!

A Lion lies in wait for Tommy - in consequence.

63 Richard Doyle
*Dick Doyle's 'Comic Histories', with the startling
story of Tommy and the Lion*
London, Pall Mall Gazette Office, 1885. 7½ × 15 in.
Line blocks of an original pencil ms.
Private collection, pp.20–21.

64 Maurice Sendak
Pierre
London, Collins, 1964 (The Nutshell Library).
3½ × 4¾ in. Photo-litho reproduction of pen-drawings
with colour-separation.
BL. cup 550/d3, pp.30–31

Two uncaring boys consumed by the same
fate. Pierre is probably not related to Tommy
by anything more than happy accident, but
the two portrayals share a complete sufficiency
of expression attained through a minimum of
graphic elaboration.

'The Nutshell Library', including *Pierre*, was
first published in New York by Harper & Row
in 1962. At the behest of librarians, larger
format editions were published later,
completely defeating the purpose, and
detracting from the charm, of Sendak's original
conception.

"I can eat you,
don't you see?"
"I don't care!"
"And you will be
inside of me."
"I don't care!"
"Then you'll never
have to bother—"
"I don't care!"
"With a mother
and a father."
"I don't care!"

8

Charles Bennett

As a forcing-ground for talent, and as media which demanded the utmost in expressive drawing, the magazines of the mid-nineteenth-century made a wonderful school for encouraging narrative art. Unfortunately however—as seems to have been the way with mid-nineteenth century schools—they were also stern taskmasters and those artists who served them needed to be resilient creatures if they were to make a way for themselves as book illustrators as well as journalists. To some extent therefore, a fund of energy that might have found its way into nursery literature runs only a subterranean course through the now obscure pages of heavily-bound periodicals. John Leech, who was, with Doyle, the leading caricaturist in the first years of *Punch*, practically never turned his genius towards children's books (**65**), for all that he expended so much charm and wit on children. And John Tenniel, who succeeded Leech, was probably put off forever after his traumatic experiences with the author of *Alice*—even though that partnership has brought him a more enduring fame than ever did 'Dropping the Pilot'.

It is to a less well-known name than these that one must turn in order to see the way in which the new cartoon-style might be successfully applied to children's books: the sad-happy figure of Charles Henry Bennett. He was nurtured in the magazine tradition, doing his first work for an obscure periodical called *The Puppet-Show* in the late 1840s, and he was eventually to become a staff member of *Punch*. But where his almost exact contemporary Richard Doyle failed to fulfil his promise through a strange loss of momentum, Charles Bennett failed through ill-health. He died in 1867 at the age of thirty-eight. [15]

During his short working life Bennett produced a number of picture books

[15] A petition on behalf of his widow and 'his eight fatherless children (soon to be increased)' was sent to the Prime Minister, the Earl of Derby, in hopes of gaining a Civil List award. It was signed by, among others, Charles Kingsley and John Everett Millais.

65 [Percival Leigh]
Jack the Giant Killer, with illustrations by [John] *Leech*

London, W.S. Orr & Co., n.d. [*c*.1844] (Comic Nursery Tales). 7 × 5 in. Wood engravings by H. Vizetelly after Leech, printed on a grey-tinted background.

A sophisticated gloss is put on the word 'nursery' in this series, which was hardly likely to go far with infants, it being rather a set of supplementary readers for the *Punch* public. (The Barham-esque verses also serve as a reminder that Leech worked with Cruikshank as an illustrator of *The Ingoldsby Legends*.) In both the full-page plates and the text drawings for *Jack the Giant Killer* one can nevertheless see what the nursery missed through John Leech's absorption in the adult market.

BL. c 58 c 1, frontispiece

which show a marked advance on the rather gawky jocularity of Alfred Crowquill, and also a variegated command of technique and style. No better examples could be given than the five books that he published in 1858, which make up the heart of his reputation as a picture-book artist. The first of these (which is really a picture book for adults) is the famous *Fables of Aesop and Others Translated into Human Nature*, which presents a series of set-piece scenes that rely on the deftness of the artist in converting contemporary characters into animal equivalents: a dashing fox ogles a large widow-crow in order to get her fortune; a studious lion is driven to frenzy by a barrel-organ-playing goat. As for the frontispiece, which shows a man being tried before a court of animals for ill-treating a horse, this may well have served as a model to Lewis Carroll (or Tenniel) for the trial scene in *Alice*.

In the children's books that are its fellows one finds a gamut from the heavy comic portraiture of *The Faithless Parrot* (**66**) to the more fluent narrative drawing of *The Frog Who Would A-Wooing Go* (**67**), the marvellous tumble of ideas in *The Old Nurse's Book of Rhymes* (p. 6) and the spiralling metamorphoses of *Greedy Jem* (**68**), a book that can be numbered among the English 'Struwwelpeters'. (It also bears a faint resemblance in its graphic scheme to Hogarth's print of 'The Weighing House', where characters revolve round a magnet, exhibiting all the graduations from Absolute Gravity to Absolute Levity. Needless to say, the ideal with Hogarth is 'horizontal or good sense'.)

Our knowledge of Charles Bennett is slender and it is not clear why he did not build more firmly on this auspicious start as a picture-book artist. His later

66 Charles H. Bennett
The Faithless Parrot, designed and narrated by Charles H. Bennett

London, G. Routledge & Co; Edmund Evans engraver & printer. n.d. [1858]. 8½ × 13½ in. Printed in line and colour from engraved wood blocks.

The story hinges on love and duplicity among household pets and possesses its own share of sophistication (a yellowback for children?). The uneven placing of the pictures, separate from the text, doesn't help either. But Bennett's jaunty draughtsmanship brings into the chromographic age the rumbustious style of picture book that had first emerged fifty years earlier.

BL. 12807 f 23, centre spread.

A Frog he would a-wooing go,
Whether his mother would let him or no.

Off he set with his opera-hat.
On the road he met with a Rat.

67 Charles H. Bennett

The Frog Who Would A Wooing Go

London, G. Routledge & Co. n.d. [1858]. 8¾ × 6¼ in. Printed in line and colour from engraved wood blocks.

From the extant colour drawings for this book it looks as though Bennett originally planned a straightforward picture-book version of the traditional ballad, with a page area only half that shown here. At some point the scheme was changed and Bennett's drawings were set two-to-a-page. The consequent muddle spoiled a treatment of the story that would have been a worthy precursor to Caldecott's classic picture book.

BL. 12807 f 24, title-page.

TRUANT TOM.

TALKATIVE TOBY.

68 Charles H. Bennett

The Sad History of Greedy Jem and all his Little Brothers; narrated, invented and drawn on the wood by Charles H. Bennett

London, George Routledge & Co. n.d. [1858].
8½ × 13½ in. Printed in line and colour from engraved wood blocks.

Struwwelpeter, and, more specifically 'Suppen-Kaspar' (**57** above) seem to have been the inspiration for *Greedy Jem*. Despite some amusing verses which offset the moral flavour a little, and despite some nice graphic touches, Bennett's routine treatment of his subjects helps to clarify Maurice Sendak's high praise for Hoffmann's more varied original.

BL. 12807 f 51 pp.7–8

books are more miscellaneous—even though they do include the nonsense illustrations for D'Arcy Thompson's *Nursery Nonsense* (1864) and *Fun and Earnest* (1865), and the elaborate comic portraits for his own alphabetic *Book of Blockheads* (p. 101). It could be, however, that he was dissatisfied with the way his work was being treated by the engraver, Edmund Evans, who printed all four of the 1858 children's books. In three of these Bennett shows himself to be fitting into the current formula for picture books in series, and in each instance his work has been sadly misrepresented in reproduction. (Some of his manuscript drawings, with colour added, are extant, and it can be seen that Evans did not measure up to Bennett's ideas.) It is significant too that no other books during his lifetime were printed in colour. If colour were required—and it appears on at least nine further occasions—it was added by hand.

9

Edmund Evans and his protegés

Whatever the reason may be for Charles Bennett's withdrawal from the booming market for picture books in the 1860s, it is much to be regretted. This was the period which saw techniques of colour-printing—whether from wood or stone—stabilise themselves. In consequence, the printers and publishers moved into the trade with a rush and seemed happy to employ anyone who could supply them with raw art-work. Pictorialism abounded—either large-scale contemporary scenes in town and country (like the 'Aunt Louisa Toy Books' of *Pussy's London Life* and *Uncle's Farmyard*), or sentimental, sub-pre-Raphaelite Biblical or faery pictures. The questing wit and lively drawing of Charles Bennett would have done much to bring zest to some very heavy image-making.

Where quality did emerge (and this may seem ironic in the light of Bennett's experience) was in the printing-shop of Edmund Evans, who, from the 1860s onward, made efforts to refine the process of mass-market colour printing and the illustrator's work on which it was founded. Some—not altogether independent—evidence for this comes from Walter Crane, who remarks in his *Reminiscences* of 1907:

Mr Evans was not only a man of business but a clever artist in water colour himself, and aided my efforts in the direction of more tasteful colouring in children's books; but it was not without protest from the publishers who thought the raw, coarse colours and vulgar designs usually current appealed to a larger public, and therefore paid better . . .

a statement which serves not only to pinpoint Evans's genuine interest in improving standards at this time but also to confirm the creative place of the trade engraver in the making of picture books. He had something of the role of the modern 'packager'—commissioning, designing, and producing the work which he passed on to the publisher to distribute and from which he (and sometimes the artist) would be paid a royalty. Crane apparently had a straight fee for the 'Walter Crane Toy Books', which sold for sixpence each, and he seems to have been rather miffed that Caldecott later argued for a royalty—which was part of the reason why *his* Toy Books sold for a shilling.

There is no gainsaying the care which Edmund Evans gave to the early print-runs of his picture books, if not always the later ones. The 'clever artist' in him recognised the need for printing techniques to match the illustrator's work as closely as possible and he was one of the pioneers in applying photographic processes to the preparation of wood-blocks. He was also sensitive to colour-values and how they could be mingled through the overprinting of tints, and he exercised great care in his choice of pigments for his inks. As a result he won, and kept, the allegiance of the artists whose work he superintended from the mid-1860s until his retirement in 1898. And—as all the textbooks and memoirs so unthinkingly put it—where children's books are concerned the greatest of these are the triumvirate of Walter Crane, Kate Greenaway and Randolph Caldecott.

Looking first at Walter Crane's picture books however, one is struck by the fact that his prolific output in the Toy Book series has greatness chiefly by comparison with what else was going on. His natural feeling for page design (which he was to rationalise in such textbooks as *Line and Form* (1900) and *of the Decorative Illustration of Books* (1896) prompted a sequence of picture books of varying dimensions, from *The Railroad Alphabet* of 1865 to *Princess*

Belle-Etoile of 1875, which contrast sharply with the 'coarse colours and vulgar designs' that—as always—ruled the market-place. Each book presented him with a test as to how he could weld text and artwork into a sequence of double-page spreads that would have elegance in themselves and cohere with all their fellows, whether the subject was the twenty-six letters of the alphabet, the few lines of 'This little pig went to market...' or, the full narrative of a fairy tale. It all gave rise to some interesting experiments in packing words, lines and blocks of colour into shapely designs (**69**).

The trouble with this kind of pattern-making however is that it inevitably leads to stasis—to a preoccupation with matters of colour and proportion—which is inimical to the business of illustrating texts. Edmund Evans shrewdly implied this when he said of Crane in his *Reminiscences*: 'The only subjects I have found he could not draw were figure subjects from everyday life, such subjects as appeared in London Society...'. In other words, what characterised the illustrative tradition from Hogarth through Rowlandson, Cruikshank, and the cartoonists was beyond the powers of Walter Crane.

There are, in fact, signs that a gift for freer draughtsmanship was among Crane's many talents. Some of his early Toy Books, which include a *Sing a Song of Sixpence*, dispense with backgrounds and give him a chance to draw with the kind of informality that he shows in his private sketches and (as we have seen) in the books he made for his children (**7**). When eventually—after consultation with Evans—he broke away from his Toy Book treadmill and produced *The Baby's Opera*, he was still deeply committed to 'the decorative page'. Nevertheless, throughout this book, and its two successors, *The Baby's Bouquet* (1878) and *The Baby's Own Aesop* (1887) there are many touches around the edges of the designs which show a true illustrator's pleasure in narrative. ('Lovely things in W. Crane's *Baby's Bucket*', commented Randolph Caldecott in a letter to his friend William Clough in 1878.)

Beside Walter Crane, Kate Greenaway seems fey and vulnerable; and in her own way she too has difficulty with 'figures from everyday life'. (She 'can't draw' said Beatrix Potter bluntly.) Her exalted reputation is almost entirely due to the entrepreneurial instincts of Edmund Evans. It was he who perceived the potential popularity of her first major book, *Under the Window* (**70**) of which he printed a first edition of 20,000 copies, much to the consternation of the publisher, the cautious George Routledge; and it was he who justified his hunch through the virtuosity of his colour printing. (There are some extraordinarily daring technical effects in *Under the Window*—especially in the juxtaposition of colours—which have defeated most overseers of its printing since Edmund Evans.)

What appealed to the public about the book (apart from its unaccustomed prettiness) was probably its strange naïvete—which rings true as part and parcel of the author-illustrator's character embodied in the book. There had never been so completely *composed* a picture book before this time and we should not lose sight of the freshness of the little sub-fenestral world that Miss Greenaway brought to life. (The truth and the freshness become immediately apparent when *Under the Window* is set against the mass of imitations that were inspired by it. Evans was hard put to it to protect the limited, but personal, talents of his find, who, when she got into difficulties, could not,

69 Walter Crane

The Baby's Opera; a book of old rhymes with new dresses . . .

London & New York, George Routledge & Sons, n.d. [1877]. 7 × 15 in. Printed in line and colour from engraved wood blocks.

Crane's flat, elegant designs might serve equally well for a nursery frieze or a set of decorative tiles. Contrast such patterning with Mervyn Peake's Romantic interpretation (**94** below).

BL. B.204, pp.44–45

[16] Except that the perceptive Japanese, aided by Margaret Maloney, Curator of the Osborne Collection at the Toronto Public Library, brought out an excellent facsimile of it in 1981.

like Crane, go off and knock up a few plaster friezes for the *nouveaux riches*.)

For all her charm and fancy, however, Kate Greenaway indeed could not draw like an illustrator. She succeeded in her first book, and its even quainter successor *Marigold Garden* (1885), by force—or rather—fleetingness of character. She coped with assignments like *Little Ann* (1883), the reprint of moral poems by Ann and Jane Taylor, by virtue of applying her quasi-Regency styling to it. But when she was confronted by the crucial test, *Mother Goose* (**71**), her weaknesses became immediately apparent. The lilt and vivacity of the nursery rhyme tradition were beyond her. As a piece of printing the book counts as one of Evans's most intriguing exercises—but no amount of hot-pressed paper and brilliant inks can disguise the lamentable slackness of Kate Greenaway's line and the dullness of her picture-making ('a lovely but antiseptic affair' says Maurice Sendak in 'Mother Goose's Garnishings'). Set it beside Charles Bennett's *Old Nurse's Book* and ponder by what quirk the one has remained in print for so long while the other is virtually unknown[16]. Ponder too the parrot-cry which undiscriminatingly reiterates that the 'Evans triumvirate' were of equal power and capacity as book illustrators. Juliana Horatia Ewing was not flattering Randolph Caldecott when she wrote to him 'I believe your work will be gathered up again and treasured by those who *know* and *love* their fellow-creatures—the world around them—and the gifts of hand and eye—when Mr Crane and Miss Greenaway are out of fashion for the mass and fatiguing to the elect!!!!!!'.

SCHOOL is over,
  Oh, what fun!
Lessons finished,—
    Play begun.
Who'll run fastest,
    You or I?
Who'll laugh loudest?—
    Let us try.

K.G.

25

70

70 Kate Greenaway

Under the Window. Pictures and Rhymes for Children . . . engraved and printed by Edmund Evans

London, George Routledge & Sons n.d. [1879]. 9¼ × 7 in. Printed in line and colour from engraved wood blocks.

The awfulness of Kate Greenaway's rhymes in *Under the Window* and *Marigold Garden* has a peculiar fascination — one never quite believes that anyone could have allowed it to happen. No such perverse excuse will do for the illustrations. The absolute lack of 'fun' in this picture (and of loud laughter and fast running) is a measure of Kate's distance from the careless animation that true artists in line could bestow on their drawings.

BL. 12805 l 7, p.25

Tom, Tom, the piper's son,
He learnt to play when he was young,
He with his pipe made such a noise,
That he pleased all the girls and boys.

K.G

71 Anon.

Mother Goose; or the old nursery rhymes. Illustrated by Kate Greenaway. Engraved and printed by Edmund Evans.

London and New York, George Routledge n.d. [1881]. 7 × 5¼ in. Printed in line and colour from engraved wood blocks.

In graphic terms *Mother Goose* is one of Evans's most arresting books. In a bold effort to match the laid papers of the eighteenth century and the hand-colouring of the early nineteenth he chose a rough paper stock. This had to be rolled smooth for printing and then dipped in water afterwards to restore its 'antique' surface. The result would have been eminently justifiable if only his artist had matched the technology and given her drawings the vibrancy and sense of movement that the Mother Goose rhymes demand.

BL. c 175 bb 34, p.47

71

10

Randolph Caldecott

In the autumn of 1878 Randolph Caldecott was invited to spend a weekend at Edmund Evans's house at Witley in Surrey, where Kate Greenaway too was a guest. (Walter Crane was probably in Italy discoursing on socialism to various titled gentry with whom he was pleased to mingle). During this convivial event they went sketching and encountered '2 fat, ugly children . . . of the porcine genus' and the experience may have led, then or at a subsequent meeting, to Caldecott producing a charming, if slightly wicked sketch in the Greenaway manner (**72**). For her part, Miss Greenaway was rueful and when, in 1882, she saw his new drawings for *Hey Diddle Diddle*, she wrote to Frederick Locker: 'They are so uncommonly clever . . . I wish I had such a mind'.

The winning candour of this praise is the more attractive for coming from an illustrator whose name was so closely linked with Caldecott's (some people even thought they were married). For while her *Under the Window*—scheduled for publication in 1878—was delayed for a year, the first of the Caldecott Toy Books were one of the successes of that autumn; and, while, in critical terms, her books were to win a constant admiration from an audience that believes that children's books are the province of thin fancy, she (like Mrs Ewing) recognised that, with *The House that Jack Built* and *The Diverting History of John Gilpin* he was reuniting a rich inventiveness with rock-solid technique. Children's picture books which for so long had been visited only fitfully by those within the great tradition were now all-too-briefly to benefit from the hand of the master.

It could be objected that, by comparison with other picture-book artists of his time, Caldecott chose an easy route for himself. Unlike Kate Greenaway he did not attempt original subjects; unlike Walter Crane he did not tackle a varied range of texts—although the less said about Crane's original stories the better. His reputation rests centrally on a group of sixteen books, all made to a similar pattern, and mostly employing texts from traditional rhymes and songs. Cowper's *John Gilpin*, two poems by Goldsmith, Foote's *Panjandrum* and *The Three Jovial Huntsmen* by Edwin Waugh are near enough to 'traditional' not to seem out of place.

What is of consequence here though is not the limited range of material and the recurrent eighteenth-century background but the varied interpretive and graphic skills which Caldecott brings to bear on them. Every theme is recognised as having a character of its own which is explored with great consistency and without reference to any previously established practice.

72 Randolph Caldecott
Drawing in the style of Kate Greenaway
*c.*1879.

reproduced from *Kate Greenaway* by M.H. Spielmann and G.S. Layard, London, A. & C. Black, 1905, p.69.

'A story is told of him that one morning, staying with her in the same country-house . . . he came down declaring that he had lost all power of working in his own style and everything came out Kate Greenaways . . .'

Thus, for instance, *John Gilpin* is treated with a kind of scrubbed realism and the *Huntsmen* with deeply affectionate satire; *Sing a Song for Sixpence, A Frog he would A-wooing Go*, and *Come Lasses and Lads* exhibit in varied ways Caldecott's famous device of introducing a pictorial sub-text to the main narrative; *The Great Panjandrum Himself* welds intentionally disparate nonsense into comic unity, and—perhaps greatest of all—the *Elegy on the Death of a Mad Dog* is indeed that. Where readers may find only comedy in the poem, Caldecott—dog-man to the bottom of his hunting boots—turns the irony on its head. Yes—the dog it was that died.

Every narrative within the Toy Books is a coherent and individual interpretation. At the same time, the parts that go to make up that interpretation are almost always executed with the utmost skill and intelligence. It is drawing that lies at the root of this—not just its exactness, but its economy too. (Henry Blackburn has been often enough cited as the source for Caldecott's *obiter dicta*: 'the art of leaving out as a science' and 'the fewer lines the less error committed'.) In working on such drawing he was certainly in the temper of his times. When he first came to London he had—literally—sat at the feet of Du Maurier, whom he then called 'the greatest master of drawing in line that we have', and in his work for the magazines he shows a flair for composition and a fastidious wit that link him to that peerless *Punch* man John Leech. With his ready embracing of past times though, in the Washington Irving illustrations and throughout the Toy Books, he turns himself into a benign disciple of Rowlandson, whose bag-wigged merchants, flouncing girls, busy children and eager dogs find an idealised milieu amid the pastures and wainscotting of Caldecott's trim world.

Nor should one detract from Caldecott's use of colour. He and Evans

73 [Samuel Foote]
The Great Panjandrum Himself [illustrated by Randolph Caldecott]
George Routledge & Sons n.d. [1885]. 8 × 9¼ in.
Wood engraving in sepia after a pen drawing.
BM 249 d.7(7) p.7

and at the same time a great she-bear,
coming down the street, pops its head
into the shop.

74 [Edwin Waugh]

Three Jovial Huntsmen [illustrated by Randolph Caldecott]

George Routledge & Sons n.d. [1880]. 9¼ × 8 in. Wood engraving in sepia after a pen drawing.

'One said it was a grindlestone, another he said "Nay;
It's nought but an' owd fossil cheese, that somebody's roll't away."
     Look ye there!'

BM 249 d.6(b) p.12

This is the Dog,
That worried the Cat,
That killed the Rat,
That ate the Malt,
That lay in the House that
    Jack built.

14

75 Randolph Caldecott

One of the 'Lightning Sketches for "The House that Jack Built"'. These were reproduced in a book of that title, introduced by Aubyn Trevor-Battye in 1899, but the present example is taken from a copy printed in *The Randolph Caldecott Treasury* edited by Elizabeth Billington, London & New York, Frederick Warne, 1978, p.169.

The sketch does indeed show all the essentials for the picture seen in its finished state at **75** above, and it is typical of the series.

76 Trad.

The House that Jack Built [illustrated by Randolph Caldecott]

George Routledge & Sons n.d. [1878]. 9⅛ × 8 in. Wood engraving in sepia after a pen drawing.
BM 249 d.6(iv) p.14

77 Trad.

A Frog He Would A Wooing Go [illustrated by Randolph Caldecott]

George Routledge & Sons n.d. [1883]. 8 × 9¼ in. Printed in line and colour from engraved wood blocks.

BM 249 d.7(2) p.15

78 Trad.

Hey Diddle Diddle and Baby Bunting [illustrated by Randolph Caldecott]

George Routledge & Sons n.d. [1882]. 8 × 9¼ in. Wood engraving in sepia after a pen drawing.

Caldecott's famous gloss on 'Hey Diddle Diddle': the tragic end to the Dish's attempted elopement with the Spoon.

BM 249 d.7(1) p.12

[17] Rodney Engen *Randolph Caldecott* (1976) p. 31, citing no authority.

79 Hallam Tennyson

Jack and the Bean-stalk. English hexameters. Illustrated by Randolph Caldecott

London, Macmillan & Co., 1886. 8½ × 7 in. Line block of an original pencil ms.
BL. 12807 ff 8, p.55

between them achieved some marvellous atmospheric domestic and landscape scenes—the high-point always being the light and airiness of the English countryside in winter. But in both the colour-plates and the sequences of sepia drawings that make a unity of the books it is Caldecott's pen that does the work. Whether he is describing (**74**) or fantasising (**73**), animating real (**76**) or imagined creatures (**77**) or household objects (**78**) he shows complete command of the drawn-line.

It is said[17] that Caldecott's widow was unhappy about the publication in 1899 of his *Lightning Sketches for 'The House that Jack Built'* (**75**) and there were doubts about the wisdom of issuing his preliminary drafts for the edition of *Jack and the Bean-stalk* that he was working on when he died (**79**). Nevertheless, evidence of this kind gave a wider proof than was hidden away in sketch-books and illustrated letters of the work that went into the creation of such apparently spontaneous entertainments. *Jack and the Bean-stalk* was to be the first step in a new direction for illustrating children's books. As with Charles Bennett, one can feel nothing but deep regret that the pioneer would not be the one to follow the road.

11

Imitation, homage, continuity

81 Horace Lennard

Romps in Town. By Harry Furniss with verses by Horace Lennard. Engraved and printed by Edmund Evans.

London, George Routledge & Sons n.d. [1885]. 9¼ × 7½ in. Printed in line and colour from wood engraved blocks.

Although Harry Furniss records admiration for Caldecott he was far too busy and ebullient a figure to be a plagiarist. The four titles in his 'Romps' series were got up by Evans in the Caldecott style. It is sobering to learn that the romping protagonists were members of Furniss's own family.

BL. 12810 dd 35, p.19

'We bought his picture books eagerly as they came out', wrote Beatrix Potter to the American librarian Jacqueline Overton, in 1942. 'I have the greatest admiration for his work—a jealous appreciation; for I think that others, whose names are commonly bracketed with his, are not on the same plane at all as artist-illustrators ...'.

The quotation serves at once to indicate how Caldecott came to be revered by his fellow-professionals in the field of book-illustration, and how immediate was his impact on the book-buyers of his day. This immediacy was not without its tiresome aspects however, and, as with Kate Greenaway, the Caldecott style swiftly became a hunting ground for jovial imitators.

The most obvious of these imitations (and they follow the Caldecott style so closely that one would think them almost actionable) are the picture books published by the lithographic houses of Thomas De La Rue (**80**) and Hildesheimer & Faulkner in the 1880s.—So far as the latter are concerned, it is not without interest that Beatrix Potter too had a brush with them in her early days. Her cypher *Journal* carries a brief account of a visit to their office where she shrewdly observes how Mr Faulkner had 'a child's book not of their publication ... [with] evident ambition to possess something of the same kind.' (Entry for May 1890 in the *Journal*, ed. L. Linder, p. 206.)

Such direct copies were not the only form of imitation. In the case of Harry Furniss, for instance, in the 'Romps' series which he illustrated to texts by Horace Lennard, we find a response that comes closer to chummy acknowledgement—and was indeed endorsed by Caldecott's printer himself (**81**). In fact, it is not surprising to find the business-like Evans on the look-out for work that he could sell alongside the famous illustrators of his stable, and the Furniss books and such experiments as Griset's *Funny Foxes* were got up in

From Sweeps in love can work be e'er expected?
And so this morn the chimneys are neglected;
Upon his knees he vainly pleads. "How dare a
Black face like you address me thus?" says Sarah.

Not altogether idle are the brushes,
When on the scene Mamma, in terror, rushes.

"Begin," says Hal;—"Aye, aye," says Mall,
    "We'll lead up 'Packington's Pound;'"
"No, no," says Noll; and so says Doll,
    "We'll first have 'Sellinger's Round.'"
    Then every man began
    To foot it round about,
And every girl did jet it, jet it,
    Jet it in and out.

80 Trad.

The Maypole. Illustrated by G.A. Konstam, E. Casella and N. Casella

London, Thos. De La Rue & Co. n.d. [1882].
9½ × 16 in. Monochrome line blocks and chromolithography.

The Maypole is a picture-book version of the ballad which Caldecott illustrated as *Come Lasses and Lads*. Although undated, it appears to have been published in 1882, two years before Caldecott's version. Nevertheless, in format, production features and graphic style it owes everything to his Toy Books and it is possible that his 1884 picture book, with its characterizations and its sub-text of the lonely fiddler, was intentionally chosen to show his imitators how he could deal with the same themes. Certainly he had no need to plagiarize *them*.

BL. 12810 d 16, pp.10–11

Come Lasses and Lads [illustrated by Randolph Caldecott]

London, George Routledge & Sons n.d. [1884].
8 × 9½ in. Printed in line and colour from wood engraved blocks.

Caldecott's maypole scene.

BM 249 d.7(8) p.10

the style of the series (**82**). And long after Caldecott's death—in more troubled times—we find Lewis Baumer using Caldecott's imagery for the purpose of political propaganda (**83**).

Even in America, sincere flattery manifested itself, at one level in popular take-offs (**85**) and at another in the foundation of a major career. Howard Pyle, who was to become one of America's most versatile illustrators of children's books, first appeared before the public with a picture book that owes a direct debt to the Caldecott model (**84**).

Of far more consequence than these varied imitations is the effect that Caldecott's example has had on illustrators down to the present time. Beatrix Potter spoke for all of them in her admiration for the vigour and economy of his draughtsmanship and she is herself a paramount example of an illustrator who learned from his technique without allowing his style to swamp her own. In her illustrated letters, her preparatory manuscripts, her pictures made for sheer enjoyment—all of which are now being so fully catalogued—we can see her mind coming to terms wth the playfulness inherent in Caldecott's visualisation of texts (**86**); and in such instances as her finished rough for *The Sly Old Cat* we have an almost perfect example of the rhythmic blending of words and pictures (**87**) in an original work 'after Caldecott'.

From her early efforts to get *The Tale of Peter Rabbit* published, Beatrix Potter gained uneasy experience of the intrusion of 'the new technology' of process and half-tone colour-printing into the making of picture books. How fortunate Caldecott was, she wrote, in the letter already quoted, 'in having his work reproduced by Edmund Evans before the advent of process colour-photography and horrible clay-faced paper . . .'.

This is not to say that 'process' necessarily represented some unusually tiresome hindrance to the fine matching of text and illustration. Up to this point there had always been problems over colour-matching and sequencing when colour was introduced into picture books and Beatrix Potter's complaint merely points to a different set of constraints. As has already been noted (p. 00 above) the camera conferred a new freedom on the artist in line, but it was paid for by the awkwardness of using a mixed paper-stock, or of printing throughout on coated paper, once colour was introduced. This led to an outcrop of rather static scene-painting from such artists as John Hassall and the Brothers Brock who were among the first illustrators to exploit the new methods in picture books of traditional tales. (Caldecott's disciple, Hugh Thomson, produced only one children's book in a 'Fairy Library' which Messrs Macmillan projected for him as a revival of the Caldecott fashion. His *Jack the Giant Killer* of 1896 was thought to be too bloodthirsty however, and he returned to his accustomed eighteenth-century pastiches.)

It was left to that devoted admirer of Caldecott, L. Leslie Brooke, to seek to achieve a full matching of text and picture in the nursery books that he produced under the new dispensation. More than anyone he saw the fun that could be derived from narrative illustration (**88,89**) and brought to his work a fluent draughtsmanship. Even here though, once he is confronted by a mix of plain and coated paper as in his own books about Johnny Crow, or in his illustrations for Lear, there is an unnatural divorce between line and colour-work (**90**).

The solution of course lay in the development of lithographic processes

ALL IN TO BEGIN!
WALK up, walk up, the *Show's* the thing!
"The Funny Foxes" in full swing.

82 Ernest Griset

The Funny Foxes and their Feats at the Fair. With sixteen illustrations by Ernest Griset. Engraved and printed by Edmund Evans.

London, Glasgow, New York, George Routledge & Sons n.d. [1887]. $7\frac{1}{4} \times 9\frac{5}{8}$ in. Printed in line and colour from wood engraved blocks.

Griset was a draughtsman of vigour and inventiveness who might have become one of Caldecott's equals in the field of picture books. However, his activities and interests led him elsewhere and this wayward excursion — perhaps commissioned by Evans after Caldecott's death — is too hastily undertaken to indicate fully the contribution that he might have made.

BL. 12811, f.50

83(a)

83(b)

19

And every time they touched it off
They scamper'd like the nation.

84

85

83 Dr [Oliver] Goldsmith

An Elegy on the Death of a Mad Dog, pictured by R. Caldecott, sung by Master Bill Primrose

London, George Routledge & Sons n.d. [1879]. 9¼ × 8 in. Printed in line and colour from engraved wood blocks.
BM. 249 d.6(5) p.14

Frederic Norton

An Elegy on the Death of a Mad Dog ... pictured by Lewis Baumer with all due respect to Dr Goldsmith and R. Caldecott

London & New York, Frederick Warne & Co. n.d. [1914]. 9 × 8 in. Line block of a pen drawing, with mechanical tinting.
BL. 11648 g 54, p.[10]

'Respect' is an appropriate word in the title of the Norton/Baumer *Elegy*, whose cover names

the book as 'The Mad Dog of Potsdam'. Their choice of Caldecott's work as a model for their lament over Germany's attack on Belgium in 1914 is inspired by affection — and is incidental testimony to the popularity of the Caldecott series.

84 Anon.

Yankee Doodle; an old friend in a new dress. Pictured by Howard Pyle

New York, printed by Dodd, Mead & Co., 1881. 10 × 9 in.

Format, page-arrangement, the use of a traditional song, the eighteenth-century settings, and the prevailing spirit of comedy all bespeak the influence of the Caldecott picture books on this 'prentice work. A year later, Dodd, Mead published another work which imitated both Caldecott and Pyle: Josephine

Pollard's *The Boston Tea Party*, illustrated by H.W. McVickar.
Private collection, pp.[18]–19

85 Trad.

The Most Popular Mother Goose Songs Illustrated. Color plates from original drawings by Mabel B. Hill

New York, Hinds, Hayden & Eldredge Inc., 1915. 9 × 10¼ in. 3-colour half-tone.

'Original' is not an appropriate word. Mabel B. Hill appears to have been primarily influenced by the French picture-book artist Maurice Boutet de Monvel, but she incorporates into her colour drawings ideas taken from other illustrators, including Caldecott and Kate Greenaway.
Private collection, p.24

86 [Beatrix Potter *et al*]
Comical Customers at the New Stores of Comical Rhymes and Stories

London, Ernest Nister ... n.d. [1896]. 9½ × 7½ in. 'Printed in Bavaria', probably both line and colour by lithography.

Five years before she published *The Tale of Peter Rabbit* Beatrix Potter sold a set of drawings to the firm of Ernest Nister with the title 'A Frog He Would A-Fishing Go'. They were furnished with dim verses by Clifton Bingham and included in this pictorial compendium, and, later in Nister's *Annual* for 1896. The drawings and the date are almost exactly mid-way between Caldecott's *Frog* of 1883 and *The Tale of Mr Jeremy Fisher* of 1906.

BL. 12809 u.21, p.45

which have now come to dominate picture-book production, and which led to the immense proliferation of picture books on an international scale in the years after the Second World War. The potential is to be seen in William Nicholson's *Clever Bill* of 1926 (**91**) and its equally admirable successor *The Pirate Twins* (see **101**) which are near-perfect examples of the wedding of words and pictures into a unified whole, and are experimental in their use of modern lithographic printing.

Early use of offset lithography is also to be seen in the first picture book by Edward Ardizzone, *Little Tim and the Brave Sea Captain* (**92**). Like Nicholson's books this story and its immediate successors not only built up a cohesive unity between what words and pictures said but (like the old engraved books) fitted the pictures into a hand-written text.

Ardizzone's picture-book art—whether based on his own texts, or on those of other writers, or on folk literature itself (**93**)—is distinguished by its reliance on a linear structure. Along with Mervyn Peake, who was a specialist in the grotesque rather than in mere caricature (**94**), he is also one of the few illustrators who has attempted a rationale of his approach. Peake, in *The Art of the Lead Pencil* (London, 1946) and in his introduction to a collection of his own drawings (London, 1949), speaks with an intensity that borders on

[18] Their wise words are echoed by Quentin Blake, who is both illustrator and head of the Illustrations Department at the Royal College of Art, in his essay 'Research from an illustrator's point of view', which is an account from the inside of how an artist organises his total response to a given text: planning individual drawings and sequences of drawings with 'a brief to elaborate to some extent or to counterpoint the text'. (*Research in illustration* [Conference proceedings] Brighton Polytechnic, 1982, p. 34.)

87 Beatrix Potter

The Sly Old Cat

London, and New York, Frederick Warne, 1971. $6\frac{1}{8} \times 4\frac{7}{8}$ in. Photo-litho reproduction of the author's holograph drawings in pen and sepia ink with water-colour tinting, dated on the final drawing 'March 20th '06'.

'But the rat jumped on the table and gave the jug a pat, and it slipped down quite tight over the head of the cat.'

The Sly Old Cat was planned as a sequel to the two panoramas of *The Fierce Bad Rabbit* and *Miss Moppet* (1906). For commercial reasons it was not completed, and when a normal book edition was discussed in 1916 Beatrix Potter felt unable to re-draw the illustrations. As a result, only her draft sketches have been published and these enable us to see not only a masterpiece in the making, but one which reflects very clearly her Caldecottian energy and wit.

BL. x998/2712, p.[25]

mysticism about the relation between the artist's vision and its representation through drawing: the need for an artist to find in an object (which may well be a text) 'the embodiment of the idea, the experience' of what it meant to the observing eye.

Ardizzone is altogether more prosaic, but in several published articles and interviews he has, like Peake, stressed the historic virtues of drawing as the *sine qua non* of illustration. 'How pretty and nicely decorated and niminy-piminy' he says of the Crane-like *art nouveau* illustrators 'compared to the robust splendours of Rowlandson, Cruikshank, Caldecott and Leech'. It is a judgment that may equally be applied to contemporary illustrative art which has tended to lose touch with traditional disciplines.[18]

For too many artists, whom the camera allowed to draw and paint pretty much as they pleased, the sobriety of illustrative work like that of Caldecott—the decent reciprocation between word and picture—seemed unambitious. Under the stimulus of modish graphic styles, often drawn from commercial art, or of fanciful central European theories about 'the education of the eye', or of an artistic free-for-all which expanded the style of the comic strip into a large-scale work, 'picture' came to be seen as the important element in the word 'picture book'. Publishers co-operating at international level for ever-larger print-runs sought glamour, rather than integrity, and were supported by the growing number of prestige-laden awards. (Even the judges for the fairly recent British Kurt Maschler Award, which seeks to honour the working-together of text and picture, have proved sadly deficient in interpreting their own terms of reference.)

Despite this pressure to be relentlessly fashionable, which produces hundreds of smart but negligible picture books every year, the tradition does

"At three," said the Wolf.

So the little Pig went off before the time, as usual, and

got to the Fair, and bought a butter churn, and was on his way home with it when he saw the Wolf coming. Then he could not tell what to do. So he got into the churn to hide, and in doing so turned it round, and it began to roll, and rolled down the hill with the Pig inside it, which frightened the Wolf so much that he ran home without going to the Fair.

continue. It is not clear how far this is due to a sanctioning of it in official art-teaching circles, but probably—as has usually been the case—it is due more to the untutored liking for making up pictures to match texts, which Edward Ardizzone sees as being the work of the 'born illustrator'. The urge to illustrate is the urge to do something which is fairly simple technically and fairly comprehensible; what will count are the less-easily assessable qualities of sympathy and organisation.

88 Anon.

The Story of the Three Little Pigs. With drawings by L. Leslie Brooke.

London, Frederick Warne & Co., n.d. [1904].

12 × 16 in. 3-colour half-tone, with line block in text.

A double-page spread showing Brooke's ability to get character and movement into his drawings.

BL. 12812 b 33, ff.[18–19]

89 Trad.

Ring O'Roses . . . with drawings by L.L. Brooke

London and New York, Frederick Warne & Co. n.d. [1922]. Panel sizes: 9 × 7½ in. Line blocks.

A nursery rhyme collection where Brooke has made classic use of the front and back endpapers for a pictorial joke.

BL. 12807 k 74, endpapers

90

90 Edward Lear
The Pelican Chorus and Other Nonsense Verses ...
with drawings by L. Leslie Brooke

London and New York, Frederick Warne & Co. n.d.
[1900]. 9 × 7¼ in. 3-colour half-tone for lithographic
reproduction.

Illustration for 'The Table and the Chair' who,
despite chilblains on their feet, take a walk
round the town. Brooke was always sensitive
to the self-sufficient quality of Lear's nonsense
songs and his efforts to accompany the poems
without wholly swamping them, while not
wholly successful, set a standard which has not
often been matched by subsequent predators.
BL. 012314 h 33, p.[48]

91 William Nicholson
Clever Bill

London, William Heinemann, 1926. 7⅛ × 9½ in. 4-
colour photo-lithography, using a variety of tonal
devices to suggest autolithography.

While, at first sight, not closely related to the
Caldecott tradition, *Clever Bill* is one of its
finest exemplars. The heavy lines, so different
from Caldecott's, are drawn with the same
assurance, and the paralleling of picture and
narrative throughout the book is masterly.

(I am grateful to Mr and Mrs Klemm for
pointing out further that Nicholson chose to
include three hitherto unpublished drawings
by Caldecott in the miscellany that he edited
with Robert Graves: a colour sketch in *The
Owl* of May 1919 and two unused drawings
for *The Queen of Hearts* in *The Winter Owl* of
1923.)
Private collection, pp.16–17

and she forgot poor *Bill Davis,* 'but

he ran

Besides helping the cook Tim would run errands and do all sorts of odd jobs, such as taking the Captain his dinner and the second mate his grog,

helping the man at the wheel, and sewing buttons on the sailor's trousers.

To those that should their Butchers be,
    And work their Lives decay.
So that the pretty speech they had,
    Made Murderers' hearts relent,
And they that took the Deed to do,
    Full sore they did repent.

Away then went those pretty Babes
    Rejoicing at that Tide,
Rejoicing with a merry mind,
    They should on Cock horse ride:
They prate and prattle pleasantly,
    As they rode on the way,

92 Edward Ardizzone

Little Tim and the Brave Sea Captain

London, New York and Toronto, Oxford University Press, 1936. 13½ × 19 in. Photo-lithographic reproduction of a colour drawing in pen and ink and water-colour. The hand-lettering is by Grace Allen Hogarth.

A double-page spread from Ardizzone's first picture book, vastly reduced from its original dimensions. Unembarrassed by the page-size that he had chosen (which may have been influenced by the success of the first 'Babar' books) he exploited it to counterpoint the verbal and the pictorial narratives.

BL. 20100 c 3, ff.[18–19]

93 Anon.

The Old Ballad of the Babes in the Wood, illustrated by Edward Ardizzone

London, The Bodley Head, 1972. 9 × 13 in. Photo-litho reproduction of pen and ink drawings.

This low-key, impressionist 'Babes in the Wood' is the only specific point of correspondence between Ardizzone and Caldecott and it stands in considerable contrast to its predecessor. Both depend upon line-drawing, but Ardizzone reverts to a visualisation that might have been found in the Regency picture books, rather than imitating Caldecott's full-blooded interpretive assault.

Private collection, pp.18–19

94 Trad.

Ride A Cock Horse and Other Nursery Rhymes. Illustrated by Mervyn Peake

London, Chatto & Windus, 1940. 10 × 7½ in. Photo-litho reproduction of a pen drawing with stencilled colour.

There is an etcher's power behind this intensely-imagined illustration for the nursery rhyme 'I Had a Little Nut Tree'. Throughout the book Peake is pressing traditional line-illustration to the limits of its expressive powers.

BL. 12812 e 54, p.[9]

94

12

A note on colour

95 William Blake
Songs of Innocence
The Author and Printer W. Blake. 1789

Three different treatments of Blake's plate for 'The Ecchoing Green' which show the extent to which he might vary the visual impression of the finished work:

(a) an uncoloured print, reproduced from the electrotype in Gilchrist (see above, **39**), showing the strength, flexibility and detail of Blake's 'wirey line';

(b) a plain, lightly-coloured version, reproduced from the Trianon Press facsimile already noted (see above, **38**) having a decorative appearance not far different from the tinting that would occur in the Regency children's picture books;

(c) a fully-coloured version, reproduced from a facsimile of *Songs of Innocence and of Experience* (coloured *c.*1825) printed in collotype and stencil and published by the Trianon Press, Clairvaux, 1955 (BL. C102.a.17, plate 6). Here the use of darker colours, of colour contrasts and of coloured decorations serves to emphasize the ominous undertones of the poem.

An attempt has been made in this essay to insist on the primacy of drawing in the English picture-book tradition. The robust quality which Edward Ardizzone saw in Rowlandson, in Cruikshank and in Caldecott was the strength and confidence with which they expressed themselves in line. What happened after that, in the way of make-up or colouration, was the icing—or the fudge-sauce—on the cake.

In the world outside this is not so true. For most lookers-at-picture-books, children and adults alike, line is just a skeleton to be fleshed out with colour. It is a transparent framework for the final picture and, the better the illustrator, the more transparent—taken-for-granted—his line will seem to be. Colour is what impresses. Colour is what brought you to hand over eighteen pence for John Harris's picture books rather than the humbler shilling.

But colour is a delusive quality. William Blake, who had a sharp eye for humbug, saw its essential danger: that by its very prominence it distracted attention from what the illustrator was able, or was not able, to express in line: 'In a Work of Art it is not Fine Tints that are required but Fine Forms. Fine Tints without Fine Forms are always the Subterfuge of the Blockhead'. ('Public Address' p. 1. Bentley II, p. 1029.)

At the same time the artist's colour-sense, his control of his medium, is imperilled by the problems of reproduction. As we have seen in the case of the unfortunate Charles Bennett, and in some of Beatrix Potter's complaints, it was all too easy for a gap to open between the illustrator's intention and the printer's execution. Just as the critic may be wise to judge the words of a picture book before ever he looks at the images, so he may be wise to treat colour as the transparent element—to see through it to the lines beneath.

Of the age before colour-printing at least it can be said that the making of coloured books was open to a good deal of flexibility—and no one demonstrates that fact better than William Blake himself. For although he honoured drawing above all else he did not therefore reject colour. Rather he saw it as a means of heightening the expression of the line, and since—in his case—illustrator and printer were one, he was able to vary or experiment with the dramatic use of colour (**95**).

Here, as in everything else, Blake is an extreme case, and the value of colour to the tradesmen of his time is probably to be seen entirely in terms of visual attraction. Almost the only thing to commend the chill formalism of *The Elegant Girl* (**13**), for instance, is the extreme elegance of the hand-colouring that adorned the scenes of her daily life; and if one compares the plain version of a typical Harris picture book with its coloured counterpart one sees that what has been added is that elusive, marginal quality 'charm' (**96**). Everything that the artist really has to say is present on the engraved plate. (And, of course, William Blake was right. In many instances from this period where neither artist nor engraver were up to much it is the charm of the colour, or even its brilliance, that hides the fact.)

As picture books grew in size, hand-colouring came to serve a useful as well as a decorative purpose. For with larger pictures on larger pages—and sometimes with a more complex articulation of forms—colour could replace shading as a means to give depth to, or differentiate features within, a drawing—and in so doing it might heighten the expressive possibilities of a scene. This is noticeable in *Struwwelpeter* and in the picture books of Alfred

95(a)

95(b)

95(c)

7
Kind Frederick.

Fatigu'd and weak upon the road,
A Woman fell beneath her load,
To aid her, Frederick quickly bends,
Her bundle takes, and arm he lends.

8
Wicked Harry.

Always devising mischief new,
Harry the cyder Spigot drew,
To him forsooth 'twas charming fun
In waste, to see the liquor run.

7
Kind Frederick.

Fatigu'd and weak upon the road,
A Woman fell beneath her load,
To aid her, Frederick quickly bends,
Her bundle takes, and arm he lends.

8
Wicked Harry.

Always devising mischief new,
Harry the cyder Spigot drew,
To him forsooth 'twas charming fun,
In waste, to see the liquor run.

96 Anon.

The Picture Gallery; or Peter Prim's Portraits
London, John Harris, 1814.

(a) Stipple engraving from the plain edition, showing how the real 'work' in the plate lies in such details of drawing as Harry's self-satisfied smirk.
BL. ch 800/111 (5), pll.7–8

(b) The same page from the coloured edition, with the relative sparseness of the foregrounded drawings 'warmed' by the addition of water-colour tints, but with no increase in the significance of the images.
Private collection, pll.7–8

97 Charles H. Bennett

The Book of Blockheads; how and what they shot, got; said, had etc . . .

London, Sampson Low & Co., 1863

Frontispiece to this alphabetic medley, which follows the subject sequence of 'A was an Archer . . .'. Comparision of the plain and coloured versions shows how colour helps to distinguish a number of the blockheads who are later to appear.

(a) Plain edition

(b) Hand-coloured edition

Both: Private collection, frontispiece

Crowquill, but it can best be exemplified in Charles Bennett's *Book of Blockheads* which was issued in coloured and uncoloured editions (**97**). The plain version shows all Bennett's delight in comedy; the coloured version clarifies and gives edge to it.

The advent of colour-printing at once introduces a more complex set of critical considerations into the assessment of picture books. The technology which made the colour revolution possible was developed during the middle decades of the nineteenth century and, in broad terms (omitting various experimental ideas), it relied upon the making of a line key-plate which could be used for building a coloured image. This plate might be of metal or wood and it would be used first as the skeleton of the picture and second, in several copies, as the base upon which the printer could determine a sequence of colour printings (basically yellow, blue and red) which would give a final picture of widely varying hues. The surface from which these colours were printed was usually either that of engraved wood-blocks, the emphasis of which could be reduced by 'tinting' (i.e. breaking up the solid surface with a set of narrow ruled lines) or of lithographic stones which would have a more 'grainy' character, and which tended to produce illustrations with a patina caused by the unbroken ink or chalk surface. In both cases it was possible to achieve colour images of exceptional delicacy, brilliance—and fidelity—but both processes also lent themselves to mass-production methods whereby illustration became essentially an in-house job: pictures for the sake of pictures, rather than because of any individual response to a text.

The development of the technology, which led to such widespread cheap colour-printing, was paralleled by developments in the publishing trade and by an expansion in the market for books of all kinds—especially picture books. A receptive public was being created through new trends in secular and Sunday education and through the greater accessibility of books in bookshops and on bookstalls, which public reciprocally inspired publishers and booksellers to greater competitive efforts.

The commercial use and the public enjoyment of illustration—most notably coloured illustration—was wrapped in with these technological and social trends, and it was probably at this point that the fact of colour came to predominate over the quality of line, or indeed the quality of texts, in general critical estimates. The great staples of popular tradition: nursery rhymes, fables, fairy stories, were fed into the hoppers of the printshops and out came a steady flow of gaudy trivia (**98**). It was enough to send one sensitive critic berserk. 'Here is a book I bought only the other day,—one of the things got

98 [Charles Perrault]
Hop O' My Thumb

London, Gall & Inglis, n.d. [1871?] (Nursery Toy Books series). Chromolitho reproduction by Kronheim & Co. of a water-colour drawing.

An example of a typical Victorian toy book where the character and quality of the illustration are subordinated to the publisher's demand for busy pages packed with colour. The artist is anonymous, but is now known to be Kate Greenaway, taking on an early commission.

University of California at Los Angeles Research Library; Dept of Special Collections, CBC H77 1871

99 William Allingham

In Fairy Land; a series of pictures from the elf-world by Richard Doyle.

London, Longmans, Green, Reader & Dyer, 1870.
Picture size 4 × 11½ in. within a page area of
10½ × 15 in. Drawing in pen and ink and water-colour printed from engraved wood blocks.

This water-lily procession appears on folio 18
of Doyle's album, with an equivocal caption
by the artist, who doesn't seem to know what
is going on. Mr Allingham's feeble verse
description is not much help either, especially
since it does not appear until folio 21, after
another group of pictures. Doyle's original was
printed by Evans from at least nine wood
blocks which, through wonderfully skilful
colour analysis and registration, convey all the
subtle hues and highlights of the scene. No
modern four-colour process (as here) can do it
justice.

BL. 1876 e.18, f.18

100 [Edwin Waugh]

Three Jovial Huntsmen [illustrated by Randolph
Caldecott]

George Routledge & Sons n.d. [1880]. 9½ × 8 in.
Printed in line and colour from engraved wood
blocks.

'One said it was a fat pig, but another he said
"Nay;
It's just a Lunnon Alderman, whose clothes are
stole away."

    Look ye there!'

Evans's loving re-creation of a full-page
Caldecott illustration. An original outline
drawing of the scene would have been made
by the artist, from which a key-block would
have been engraved. He would then have
coloured-in a pull from this for the making of
the colour blocks: buff, blue, grey and red. This
restrained, naturalistic use of colour enhances
rather than clouds what the artist has to say.

BL. 12805 s 17, p.[23]

how to dance

and how to play

101 William Nicholson

The Pirate Twins

London, Faber & Faber, 1929. 7 × 19 in. Pen and ink and water-colour drawing screened for reproduction by litho.

As in *Clever Bill* (**91** above) Nicholson here achieves maximum expression with a minimum of means. Neither his palette nor the amount of colour that he uses is extensive but it is ideally suited for lithographic reproduction.
BL. 012804 d6 43 pp.14–15

102 Beatrix Potter

The Tale of Mrs Tittlemouse

London and New York, Frederick Warne & Co., 1910. 5¾ × 4¼ in. Pen and sepia ink drawing with water-colour, reproduction by line and three-colour half-tone (yellow blue and red).

Here too the lightness and precision of the artist's drawing is complemented by her use of colour — but the finished print is muddied by the screening of the colours needed for half-tone reproduction, and by the glossy paper which the process required.
BL. Cup 402 a.13, p.81

103 Ruth Craft

The Winter Bear, illustrated by Erik Blegvad

London, Collins, 1974. 8 × 7¾ in. Photo litho reproduction of a pen and ink drawing with water-colour.

'Knitted with care.
A bit damp, a bit leafy,
In need of repair,
But still, an excellent bear . . .'

Ruth Craft's graceful text about the rescuing of the Winter Bear is perfectly matched by Erik Blegvad's affectionate, atmospheric water-colours. At any moment three jovial huntsmen could come charging over the next hill.
BL. x990/17839 p.[16]

[19] Alas that the Master did not give bibliographical details. Heaven forfend that he was holding up Walter Crane to such obloquy, but Crane's Sixpenny Toy Book of c.1873 does correspond. And heaven forfend even more that he was talking about the *Puss in Boots* that his much-loved Kate Greenaway once illustrated for a cheap Gall & Inglis toy-book series.

[20] The drawings are still in existence, and are now in a private collection. Several years ago I was able to compare them with a copy of Evans's book and observe how admirably he had captured the nuances of Doyle's colouring.

[21] Maurice Sendak has recalled how—as a judge at the Biennale of Children's Book Illustration at Bratislava in 1970—he found himself trying to make a case for such artists as Edward Ardizzone against the overwhelming bias in favour of expressionist *Wunderkinder* from central European art-schools or masters of Japanese design.

up cheap to catch the eyes of mothers at bookstalls,—Puss in Boots, illustrated; a most definite work of the colour school—red jackets and white paws and yellow coaches as distinct as Giotto or Raphael would have kept them. But the thing is done by fools for money, and becomes entirely monstrous and abominable'. (John Ruskin. *Ariadne Florentina*. Fasc. I (1873), p. 24).[19]

At the other end of the spectrum things were not necessarily any better. One of the most majestic examples of trade colour-printing in Victorian times is surely *In Fairy Land*, which Edmund Evans printed for Longmans in 1869 (dated 1870). The book was a brilliant reproduction of a set of water-colour drawings by Richard Doyle, printed in anything from eight to (probably) twelve colours [20] (**99**)—but it was nothing else. Nobody knew what to do with this *tour de force* and it ended up by being issued as a fancy album of images, set in a loose relationship with each other through some dim, *post facto* versifying by William Allingham. (Later on the pictures were split up in various ways and used with an equally dim *post post facto* story, *The Princess Nobody*, by Andrew Lang.)

These two examples may stand for the fate of much illustration at the hands of the colour-merchants. As we have seen though, it was the good fortune of Randolph Caldecott to come into association with a printer of Evans's skill, so that when the occasion did arise for publishing works that brought together the illustrator's sense of line and colour and his responsiveness to texts the means were available to do them justice. Evans's use of key blocks to supply Caldecott with line-proofs, which he could use to create a guide for the making of colour-blocks, and Evans's careful application of tint-tools and properly chosen inks, ensured that the colours in the Toy Books measured up to the artist's conception (**100**).

The reticence of Caldecott's colouring in most of these books—his refusal to allow the truth of his line to be compromised by chromatic extravagance—may well be the chief reason why his books have fallen from public favour (aided and abetted by the decreasing care given to their production by their publisher). The passion of Ruskin's outburst against chromo-lithography stemmed, as much as anything, from his frustrated recognition that the public (including children) needs must love the lowest—or the brashest—when they see it.

In the hundred years that have followed Caldecott's death it has always been difficult for the reticent geniuses to stand against the heavy colourists or the fanciful makers of collages, etc.[21] Even Beatrix Potter, who is now the subject of one of the most intensive selling-campaigns ever devised for an author, is in danger of having her true worth neglected behind piles of crockery, greetings-cards, birthday-books, and re-illustrated editions of her masterpieces. For although she had to contend against the inhibitions of tri-chromatic printing (by which her colour drawings were converted into colour-blocks by the use of photographic filters), she never lost sight of the fact that her books were a unity of story and line; the colour was there for decoration or atmosphere (**102**). It was the contrast and the vigour of the drawing that mattered—Caldecottian touchstones, 'the sense of music and dance'—as valid now as over the two hundred and fifty years that they have been part of our graphic tradition.

13

Coda: Bread and Honey

To make choices among the welter of moderately acceptable picture books that spin from the presses today is rather invidious. By way of compromise therefore a few examples are given here to show the vigour of recent, or fairly recent, work. They have been selected not necessarily as 'the best' of modern picture books (by the standards that we learn from Caldecott) but as representatives of different thematic groups within the general category of 'nursery literature'. Faced with a variety of interpretive exercises the artists have found satisfying answers:

104 A Nursery Rhyme Picture Book

Trad. *Hector Protector and As I Went Over the Water; two nursery rhymes with pictures by Maurice Sendak*

London, Sydney, Toronto, The Bodley Head, 1967. 7¼ × 16½ in. Photo-litho reproduction of a pen and wash drawing.

Sendak has written that 'Caldecott gave me my first demonstration of the subtle use of rhythm and structure in a picture book' and that *Hector Protector* was 'an intentionally contrived homage to this beloved teacher'. The homage lies less in any imitative transaction than in the idea of using two brief nursery rhymes as a prompt for more elaborate pictorial narratives.

The book was first published in New York by Harper & Row in 1965.

BL. x998/1168, pp.[18–19]

105 A Nursery Story

John Burningham. *Mr Gumpy's Outing*

London, Jonathan Cape, 1970. 10 × 20 in. Photo-litho reproduction of drawings using mixed media, chiefly pen, coloured inks, crayon and water-colour.

One of the classics of modern picture-book art, reminiscent of Caldecott both in its balanced used of line and colour and in the natural ease with which story and illustration move forward together.

BL. cup 24 e 46, pp.[14–15]

106 A Play Book

Janet and Allan Ahlberg. *Each Peach Pear Plum*

London, Kestrel Books, 1978. 7½ × 19¼ in. Photo-litho reproduction of a pen and ink drawing with water-colour.

While each page opening has a charm of its own, the full beauty of this book lies in the cumulative sequence of images: the 'reader' seeking in one picture what is to be the subject of the next. And at the end, everyone meets for a grand plum-pie picnic . . .

BL. Cup 1281/920, pp.[12–13]

107 A Nonsense Rhyme

Quentin Blake. *Mr Magnolia*

London, Jonathan Cape, 1980. 10¼ × 8 in. Photo-litho reproduction of a drawing in pen and ink.

The farcical text, which makes play with the number of rhymes that can be found for 'boot', is perfectly matched by the drawing. Blake's apparently spontaneous pen-work has a rhythm and expressiveness that depend upon a gift for observation that is anything but casual.
BL. x992/3985, p.[7]

108 An American Parallel

Arnold Lobel. *Frog and Toad Are Friends*

Kingswood, The World's Work, 1971; first published in New York by Harper & Row in 1970. 8⅛ × 5¾ in.

Arnold Lobel is one of the most fluent and sensitive illustrators at present creating picture books in the United States. He has a natural flair — backed up by a command of drawing — for finding the illustrative response that is right for each individual text. In the 'Frog and Toad' books he uses subdued, small water-colours to complement his wryly humorous stories. In *The Man Who Took the Indoors Out* he works with a stronger medium to make a book that must surely have been influenced by Edward Lear.

BL. x990/2845, p.39

109 An American Parallel

Harve Zemach. *The Judge; an untrue tale, with pictures by Margot Zemach.*

London, Sydney, Toronto, The Bodley Head, 1970. 7⅞ × 19¾ in. Photo-litho reproduction of a drawing in pen and ink and water-colour.

Maurice Sendak is not the only artist in the United States to admire the English tradition in illustration. Here one of Sendak's great contemporaries illustrates a cumulative verse-comedy with pictures reminiscent of Rowlandson.

BL. Cup 24.g.32, pp.40–41

110 An Alphabet Book

Colin McNaughton. *ABC and Things.*

London, Ernest Benn, 1976. 6 × 14 in. Photo-litho reproduction of a pen and water-colour drawing.

A cleverly worked-out text, harking back to *Peter Prim's Pride* (**47**), which gives literal interpretations of current sayings

BL. x990/8852, pp.20–21

111 Arnold Lobel. *The Man Who Took the Indoors Out.*

Kingswood, The World's Work, 1976; first published in New York by 1974. 9¼ × 7½ in.
BL. x990/7401

But Mr Magnolia has only one boot.

107

The next day Toad gave
his jacket to Frog.
Frog thought that it was beautiful.
He put it on and jumped for joy.
None of the buttons fell off.
Toad had sewed them on very well.

39

108

109

T
is for Too big for his boots

110

111

Encore:
Sing a Song
for Sixpence

By way of conclusion there follow
here a number of examples of
illustrations for the nursery rhyme
that (in Caldecott's wording) gave
a title to the exhibition.

from: *The Old Nurse's Book of Rhymes, Jingles and Ditties*, edited and
illustrated by Charles H. Bennett. London, Griffith & Farran, 1858

Sing a Song of Sixpence. Edinburgh,
W. P. Nimmo n.d. [*c*.1872]
(Marcus Ward's Royal Illuminated Nursery
Rhymes series)

Sing a Song of Sixpence [illustrated by·
Walter Crane] London, George Routledge
& Sons n.d. [1886] (Aunt Mavor Toy Books
series)

from a manuscript published in
*Queery Leary Nonsense; a Lear
nonsense book*; edited by Lady Strachey.
London, Mills & Boon, 1911

Sing a Song for Sixpence. One of R.
Caldecott's Picture Books.
London, George Routledge
& Sons n.d. [1880]

A drawing by John Ward, aged 6,
of Dewhurst St. Mary's JMI
School, Cheshunt, Hertfordshire.

Bibliography

Caldecott's 'House that Jack Built' in L. Leslie Brooke's illustration for that rhyme in *The Nursery Rhyme Book* 'edited' by Andrew Lang (London, Frederick Warne & Co., 1897)

Most of the following works include information about children's picture books. It is not always as detailed or accurate as one would wish, but the books, with their own bibliographies, will serve as a point of departure for readers wishing to explore further.

General Works

David Bland. *The history of book illustration; the illuminated manuscript and the printed book.* Second ed., London, Faber & Faber, 1969

David Bland. *The illustration of books.* Third ed., London, Faber & Faber, 1962.

Rodney K. Engen. *Dictionary of Victorian wood engravers.* Cambridge, Chadwyck-Healey, 1985

William Feaver. *When we were young...* London, Thames & Hudson, 1977

Martin Hardie. English coloured books. London, Methuen, 1906 (The Connoisseurs Library); reissued with an intro. by James Laver, Bath, Kingsmead, 1973

Simon Houfe. *The dictionary of British book illustrators and caricaturists 1800–1914; with introductory chapters on the rise and progress of the art.* Woodbridge, Antique Collectors Club, 1978

Bertha E. Mahony et al. *Illustrators of children's books 1744–1945.* Boston, The Horn Book Inc., 1947
(With three subsequent volumes covering the decades 1946–1976.)

Percy Muir. *English children's books 1600–1900.* London, Batsford, 1954

Percy Muir. *Victorian illustrated books.* London, Batsford, 1971

Iona and Peter Opie. *Three centuries of nursery rhymes and poetry for children* [Exhibition catalogue]. London, National Book League, 1973

Gordon N. Ray. *The illustrator and the book in England from 1790 to 1914.* New York, Pierpont Morgan Library, 1976

Janet Adam Smith. *Children's illustrated books.* London, Collins, 1948 (Britain in Pictures series)

Mary Thwaite. *From primer to pleasure in reading...* second ed. London, Library Association, 1972

Uncalled-for modesty in this delightful acknowledgment by Wallace Tripp in his *Rhymes Without Reason from Mother Goose* (Kingswood, The World's Work, 1978; first published in New York as *Granfa' Grig Had a Pig...* Little, Brown, 1976).

Critical prompts and studies

Brian Alderson. *Looking at picture books 1973. An exhibition...* London, National Book League, 1973

Barbara Bader. *American picture books from Noah's Ark to The Beast Within.* New York, Macmillan, 1976

Edward Hodnett. *Image and text; studies in the illustration of English literature.* London, Scolar Press, 1982
(No reference to picture books, but valuable for its discussion of principles.)

Maurice Sendak. *Mother Goose's garnishings. Book Week no.31;* reprinted in *Children's literature; views and reviews,* ed. Virginia Haviland. Glenview, Ill., Scott, Foresman, 1973

Sacheverell Sitwell. *Narrative pictures; a survey of English genre and its painters...* London, Batsford, 1938

R.E.D. Sketchley. *English book illustration of today; appreciations of the work of living illustrators with lists of their books.* London, Kegan Paul, Trench, Trubner & Co. 1903

Lillian H. Smith. *The unreluctant years...* Chicago, American Library Association, 1953
(Chapter 8 is on 'Picture Books'.)

Dorothy Neal White. *Books Before five.* Auckland, New Zealand Council for Educational Research; Oxford University Press, 1954

Technical matters

R. M. Burch. *Colour printing and colour printers; with a chapter on modern processes by W. Gamble.* Second ed. London, Pitman, 1910

Joan M. Friedman. *Color printing in*

See, see! What shall I see?
A horse's head where his tail should be.

Trina Schart Hyman inscribes 'Apologies to R.C.' in the corner of this introductory scene for *On to Widecombe Fair* by Patricia Lee Gauch (Kingswood, The World's Work, 1979).

England 1484–1870. An exhibition... New Haven, Yale Center for British Art, 1978

Lynton Lamb. *Drawing for illustration.* London, Oxford University Press, 1962

C.T. Courtney Lewis. *The story of picture printing in England during the nineteenth century; or forty years of wood and stone.* London, Sampson Low, Marston & Co., n.d. [1924]

Ruari McLean. *Victorian book design and colour printing.* Second ed. London, Faber & Faber, 1972

Geoffrey Wakeman. *Victorian book illustration; the technical revolution.* Newton Abbot, David & Charles, 1973

General works and studies about individual artists etc.

BARLOW
Edward Hodnett. *Francis Barlow, first master of English book illustration.* London, Scolar Press, 1978

HOGARTH
Ronald Paulson. *Hogarth's graphic works.* Second ed. New Haven, Yale University Press, 1970

ROWLANDSON
Ronald Paulson. *Rowlandson; a new interpretation.* London, Studio Vista, 1972

BLAKE
William Blake's Writings, ed. G.E. Bentley Jr. 2 vols. Oxford, Clarendon Press, 1978

William Blake. *The notebook; a photographic and typographic facsimile*, ed. David V. Erdman... Oxford, Clarendon Press, 1973

G.E. Bentley Jr. *Blake books; annotated catalogues of W.B.'s writings...* Oxford, Clarendon Press, 1977

Zachary Leader. *Reading Blake's 'Songs'.* London, Routledge, 1981

BEWICK
Iain Bain. *The watercolours of Thomas Bewick and his workshop apprentices.* 2 vols. London, Gordon Fraser, 1981

THE 'HARRIS' BOOKS etc
Marjorie Moon. *John Harris's books for youth 1801–1843; a check-list.* Richmond, North Yorkshire, Five Owls Press [for the compiler] 1976. With a supplement, 1983

Iona and Peter Opie. *A nursery companion.* Oxford University Press, 1980

CRUIKSHANK
Albert M. Cohn. *George Cruikshank; a catalogue raisonée... 1806–1877.* London, The Bookman's Journal, 1924

William Feaver, intro. *George Cruikshank* [Exhibition catalogue] London, Arts Council of Great Britain, 1974

LEAR
Vivien Noakes. *Edward Lear 1812–1888...* [Exhibition catalogue] London, Royal Academy of Arts, 1985

DOYLE
Rodney Engen. *Richard Doyle.* Stroud, Catalpa Press, 1983

EVANS
The reminiscences of Edmund Evans, ed. Ruari McLean. Oxford, Clarendon Press, 1967

CRANE
Walter Crane. *An artist's reminiscences.* London, Macmillan, 1907

Isobel Spencer. *Walter Crane.* London, Studio Vista, 1975

GREENAWAY
M. H. Spielmann & G. S. Layard. *Kate Greenaway.* London, A. & C. Black, 1905

Rodney Engen. *Kate Greenaway; a biography.* London, Macdonald, 1981

GRISET
Lionel Lambourne. *Ernest Griset...* London, Thames & Hudson, 1979

CALDECOTT
Elizabeth T. Billington ed. *The Randolph Caldecott treasury... with an appreciation by Maurice Sendak.* London, Warne, 1978

Rodney K. Engen. *Randolph Caldecott...* London, Oresko Books, 1976

Michael Hutchins, ed. *Yours pictorially; illustrated letters of R. C.* London, Warne, 1976

POTTER
Leslie Linder. *A history of the writings...* London, Warne, 1971

Anne Stevenson Hobbs & Joyce Irene Whalley... *Beatrix Potter; the V & A collection.* London, Victoria & Albert Museum... 1985

BROOKE
Henry Brooke. *Leslie Brooke and Johnny Crow.* London, Warne, 1984

ARDIZZONE
Brian Alderson. *Edward Ardizzone; a preliminary hand-list... 1929–1970.* Pinner, The Private Library, 1972

Gabriel White. *Edward Ardizzone; artist and illustrator.* London, Bodley Head, 1979

SENDAK
Selma Lanes. *The art of Maurice Sendak.* London, Bodley Head, 1981

Yet another Sendak reference. The tiny letters 'R.C.' are embroidered in the corner of the rear horseman's saddle-cloth. From 'The Huntsmen' in *Lullabies and Night Songs*, edited by William Engvick, with music by Alec Wilder and pictures by M.S. (New York, Harper & Row, 1965; London, The Bodley Head, 1969).

Index

(1) Dates have been given for all major artists etc. Books are always dated in the captions.

(2) A slash between page numbers indicates that pages of illustration lie between the text pages.

(3) References to illustrations are in bold type. Where these are followed by 'c' it indicates that the subject is dealt with in the caption.

'The Caldecott Memorial' drawn by F.D. Bedford for one of the picture books that he made in collaboration with E.V. Lucas: *A Visit to London.*